VIVA Bloom's NOTES

Joseph Conrad's HEART OF DARKNESS & THE SECRET SHARER

Edited and with an Introduction by

HAROLD BLOOM

Viva Books Private Limited
New Delhi • Mumbai • Chennai • Kolkata • Bangalore • Hyderabad

First Indian Edition 2007

VIVA BOOKS PRIVATE LIMITED

- 4737/23 Ansari Road, Daryaganj, New Delhi 110 002
E-mail: vivadelhi@vivagroupindia.net, Tel. 42242200
- Plot No. 76, Service Industries, Shirvane, Sector 1, Nerul, Navi Mumbai 400 706
E-mail: vivamumbai@vivagroupindia.net, Tel. 27721273, 27721274
- Jamals Fazal Chambers, 26 Greams Road, Chennai 600 006
E-mail: vivachennai@vivagroupindia.net, Tel. 28290304, 28294241
- B-103, Jindal Towers, 21/1A/3 Darga Road, Kolkata 700 017
E-mail: vivakolkata@vivagroupindia.net, Tel. 22836381, 22816713
- 7, Sovereign Park Apartments, 56-58, K. R. Road, Basavanagudi, Bangalore 560 004
E-mail: vivabangalore@vivagroupindia.net, Tel.26607409, 26607410
- 101-102 Mughal Marc Apartments, 3-4-637 to 641, Narayanguda, Hyderabad 500 029
E-mail: vivahyderabad@vivagroupindia.net, Tel. 27564481, 27564482

Published by arrangement with

Facts on File, Inc.
132 West 31st Street
New York NY 10001
USA

ISBN 81-309-0446-2

Published by Vinod Vasishtha for Viva Books Private Limited, 4737/23 Ansari Road
New Delhi 110 002. Printed and bound at Anand Sons, Delhi.

Contents

User's Guide

This volume is designed to present biographical, critical, and bibliographical information on Joseph Conrad, *Heart of Darkness,* and "The Secret Sharer." Following Harold Bloom's introduction, there appears a detailed biography of the author, discussing the major events in his life and his important literary works. Then follows a thematic and structural analysis of the works, in which significant themes, patterns, and motifs are traced. An annotated list of characters supplies brief information on the chief characters in the works.

A selection of critical extracts, derived from previously published material by leading critics, then follows. The extracts consist of such things as statements by the author on his works, early reviews of the works, and later evaluations down to the present day. The items are arranged chronologically by date of first publication. A bibliography of Conrad's writings (including a complete listing of books he wrote, cowrote, edited, and translated in his lifetime, and important posthumous publications), a list of additional books and articles on him and on *Heart of Darkness* and "The Secret Sharer," and an index of themes and ideas conclude the volume.

Harold Bloom is Sterling Professor of the Humanities at Yale University and Henry W. and Albert A. Berg Professor of English at the New York University Graduate School. He is the author of twenty books and the editor of more than thirty anthologies of literature and literary criticism.

Professor Bloom's works include *Shelley's Mythmaking* (1959), *The Visionary Company* (1961), *Blake's Apocalypse* (1963), *Yeats* (1970), *A Map of Misreading* (1975), *Kabbalah and Criticism* (1975), and *Agon: Towards a Theory of Revisionism* (1982). *The Anxiety of Influence* (1973) sets forth Professor Bloom's provocative theory of the literary relationships between the great writers and their predecessors. His most recent books are *The American Religion* (1992) and *The Western Canon* (1994).

Professor Bloom earned his Ph.D. from Yale University in 1955 and has served on the Yale faculty since then. He is a 1985 MacArthur Foundation Award recipient and served as the Charles Eliot Norton Professor of Poetry at Harvard University in 1987–88. He is currently the editor of the Chelsea House series Major Literary Characters and Modern Critical Views, and other Chelsea House series in literary criticism.

Introduction

HAROLD BLOOM

Marlow, the narrator of most of *Heart of Darkness,* also may be the teller of "The Secret Sharer," though he is not named there. Far more overtly Romantic than his author and other self, Joseph Conrad, Marlow worships, and to some extent exemplifies, courage. Conrad distances himself from Marlow, sometimes with considerable irony, but allows his mariner-narrator to be very likable if in some ways limited by his elitism of "knowing" who is and is not "one of us." Like the subtle Conrad, Marlow is a moralist, but he tends to be rather more confused than Conrad generally allowed himself to be. *Heart of Darkness,* more than the other famous works of Conrad, raises doubts in some critics about the novelist's own clarity. There is a lingering obscurantism in *Heart of Darkness* that may render it less than fully coherent. Most accounts of the short novel's "meaning" tend to give us something that is just not quite there in the text. It may be that the almost universal of *Heart of Darkness* relies upon this wavering of authentic significance in the story. T. S. Eliot, Hemingway, Scott Fitzgerald, and Faulkner all were indebted to *Heart of Darkness,* as have been a sequence of American filmmakers from Orson Welles to the Coppola of *Apocalypse Now.* The language of the story, whether it be Marlow's or the other narrator's, tends to be imprecise. It is as though neither Marlow nor Conrad really knows what the narration talks about, particularly when the nature of Kurtz is the prime issue. Kurtz means too many things, or too few, sometimes simultaneously, and his story never gets quite told.

Heart of Darkness survives this obscurantism, not so much because of the central figure of Kurtz, but because the quest element of journeying to the interior is managed so well, both by Conrad and by Marlow. Going up the river becomes so urgent a metaphor that the reader scarcely is able to resist it. Kurtz, supposed to be supremely articulate, is muted by Marlow, evidently unaware of this effect. The journey matters more than the destination; you achieve a courageous aura by the quest, even though the object of your quest is a blank or an emptiness. Whether this apparent irony is part of Conrad's design is not clear. The odd achievement is that a moral voyage is divested of its purpose, and we continue to be enthralled, because we participate in an enhancement of consciousness, Marlow's, though we are uncertain just what it is that Marlow has learned.

"The Secret Sharer," equally persuasive as narrative, oddly has the opposite demerit: there clearly *is* a fable, and it is schematically presented, with a neatness that is a touch disheartening. When the captain's hat, given by him to Leggatt, the secret sharer, returns on the water as a marker by which the ship and its captain are saved, the symbolism seems mechanical. Kurtz may or may not be Marlow's "other self"; Leggatt is nothing but the Marlow-like captain's alter ego. Yet the tale survives Conrad's excessive intentionality of meaning, primarily because it is one of the most effective rituals of initiation in all of literature. The reader, identifying with the captain, undergoes the ordeal of testing that a first command constitutes. And the language, so frequently murky in *Heart of Darkness,* takes on a continuous eloquence and accuracy that is sustained in every paragraph of the story. The Conrad of *Nostromo, The Secret Agent, Under Western Eyes,* and *Victory* is a greater writer than the tale-teller of *Heart of Darkness* and "The Secret Sharer," but they remain permanently valuable (if flawed) introductions to his artistry. ✣

Biography of Joseph Conrad

Joseph Conrad was born Józef Teodor Konrad Nalecz Korzeniowski on December 3, 1857, near Berdichev in the Ukraine, a region that had once been part of Poland but was then ruled by Russia. His parents, Apollo and Evelina Bobrowski Korzeniowski, belonged to the educated, land-owning Polish gentry and fought for Polish independence. In 1862, Apollo Korzeniowski, a talented writer and translator, was exiled to Vologda in northern Russia. The difficult life there took its toll on the family, as Conrad's mother died in 1865 and his father in 1869. Conrad moved to Kraków, Poland, to live with his maternal uncle. He spent much of his time reading Charles Dickens and Victor Hugo but also dreamed of sailing the seas.

In October 1874, Conrad received his uncle's permission to enter the French merchant marine. While learning seamanship in Marseille, he led a wild life, full of romantic adventures and reckless spending. He made three voyages to the West Indies and in his spare time engaged in gunrunning for the Carlist faction in Spain. In 1878, he shot himself (although he claimed he had been wounded in a duel); after recovering and settling his debts with his uncle's help, he sailed out of Marseille on the English freighter *Mavis.*

Knowing just a few words of English, Conrad joined the English merchant navy. Over the next sixteen years, he prospered as a seaman, visiting ports in Australia, South America, India, Borneo, and the South Pacific, among other places. In 1886, he achieved several important milestones: he was made the master of his own ship, became a British subject, and changed his name to Joseph Conrad. Traveling to Africa in 1890, he ventured up the Congo River with the Belgian colonial service. There he contracted malaria, which plagued him for years.

As a result of ill health and his growing interest in writing, Conrad retired from his seafaring career in 1894 and settled permanently in England. A year later he published his first novel, *Almayer's Folly.* The story, based on a Dutch trader Conrad had known in Borneo, garnered praise from such literary luminaries as H. G. Wells and Henry James; Conrad became friends with many of the leading writers of his day and even collaborated with Ford Madox Ford on two novels, *The Inheritors* (1901) and *Romance* (1903). In 1896, he published *An Outcast of the Islands,* also set in Borneo, and married Jessie George, with whom he later had two sons. During the next two years he published *The Nigger of the "Narcissus,"* which used poetic realism to describe the negative effects of one man upon a ship's crew, and *Tales of Unrest.*

Although he struggled financially and was racked with self-doubt about his creative ability, Conrad produced books of remarkable artistry, infusing adventure stories with profound explorations of the conflicts between and within men. His masterful novel *Lord Jim* (1900), which was inspired by a story he heard of a ship crew's desertion, brilliantly illustrates the plight of a man who had imagined himself a hero but fails when tested by dangerous circumstances; the man then devotes his life to trying to appease his conscience and recover his honor. Besides the novel *Typhoon,* in 1902 he also published the collection *Youth,* which contained *The End of the Tether* and *Heart of Darkness* (first published in *Blackwood's Edinburgh Magazine* for February, March, and April 1899) in addition to the title story. *The End of the Tether* relates the bleak tale of a man who lived an honorable life but died in loneliness. *Heart of Darkness,* which drew upon his trip up the Congo, journeys into the savage nature behind men's civilized manners.

Around this time, Conrad shifted his focus from the stirring forces at sea to the turbulence of politics. With *Nostromo* (1904), he created a fictional South American country to illustrate the frustrating futility of man's efforts at change. *The Secret Agent* (1907) describes an anarchist bomb plot in London. *Under Western Eyes* (1911) depicts the Russian autocracy in a tale of betrayal and a search for redemption.

Conrad remained prolific until the end of his life. He published autobiographical reminiscences in *The Mirror of the Sea* (1906) and *A Personal Record* (1912). The stories "The Secret Sharer" (first published in *Harper's Monthly Magazine* for

August and September 1910; collected in *'Twixt Land and Sea,* 1912) and *The Shadow-Line* (1917) were also semiautobiographical. In 1913, Conrad finally achieved popular success in England and the United States with *Chance;* after years of critical acclaim, he at last secured a measure of financial security and fame. He followed this with *Victory* (1915), *The Arrow of Gold* (1919), and *The Rescue* (1920). His last novel, *The Rover* (1923), was a French Revolution drama, and his final work, *Last Essays,* was a nonfiction collection published posthumously in 1926. Conrad died on August 3, 1924, at Bishopsbourne, Kent.

Joseph Conrad is now recognized as one of the great British novelists and short story writers of his time. *Heart of Darkness* has inspired an entire library of critical analysis. In 1979 Francis Ford Coppola consciously modeled his film *Apocalypse Now* on the work, with Marlon Brando as Kurtz and Martin Sheen as Captain Willard (filling the role of the narrator Marlow). "The Secret Sharer" has also been adapted as a short film. Conrad's letters have been published, and in 1989 Cambridge University Press began the issuance of a new, authoritative edition of his *Works* under the general editorship of S. W. Reid. ✣

Thematic and Structural Analysis

Heart of Darkness begins on the Thames with a scene, peacefully unremarkable except for the dark air "brooding . . . over the biggest, and the greatest, town on earth." The first significant association of darkness to civilization is established in these preliminary passages, besides situating the outer framework of this narrative. Anchored and waiting to set sail is the *Nellie,* on which the outer narrative takes place. Aboard the *Nellie* are five acquaintances who share "the bond of the sea." There is the captain, actually a Director of Companies, a lawyer, an accountant, Marlow, and the narrator. As they wait for the tide to turn, the brilliance of the end of the day is noted and contrasted with the "gloom brooding over a crowd of men." Musing upon the view of the Thames, the narrator recollects the men who have previously sailed on it, "the men of whom the nation is proud," citing as examples Sir Francis Drake and Sir John Franklin, a revealing statement about the nation's temperament: although both Drake and Franklin were knights in name, Drake was known for being little better than a pirate, while Franklin, who never returned from his expedition, was driven by similar material interests. The sun sets, and the Thames is lit by "a great stir of [ships'] lights"; yet again, the "brooding gloom" hanging over what is now referred to as "the monstrous town" is mentioned, and Marlow recalls that it, also, was once "one of the dark places of the earth." Evoking images of the wilderness of the marshes and forests and the savagery of the wild men that must have been, Marlow draws a subtle parallel between Roman imperialism and English colonialism, but differentiates sheer "robbery with violence" from "conquest of the earth" redeemed by "an idea at the back of it."

This parallel inspires Marlow to begin a tale about one of his "inconclusive experiences" and marks a relationship between the central narrative on the Thames and the following inner narrative on the river to the heart of darkness. Back in London after a few years on the eastern seas, he is wandering about, looking for something to do. A map he notices in a shop window reminds him of the blank white spaces that represented unexplored regions in his boyhood years. The largest one, which had most excited his imagination, has since been filled with names of cities, rivers, and lakes and "had become a place of darkness." Still, he is fascinated by a snakelike river winding through the continent, and using the influences of an aunt, obtains a position as a steamboat skipper with "a big concern, a company for trade on that river." The position becomes available through portentous circumstances: Marlow's predecessor, Fresleven, "the gentlest, quietest creature," beats a village chief and himself gets killed.

Marlow's visit to the Company's headquarters is no more promising. The headquarters are silent and deserted, he is greeted by two silent women knitting black wool (reminiscent of the Fates weaving), and there is the uncomfortable ceremony of having to sign a contract. In addition, a clerk who enthuses about the Company's glorious business, which is, ironically, "to run an oversea empire, and make no end of coin by trade," conversely alludes to the foolishness of the adventurers "out there," as does a Company doctor who nonchalantly asks if there is any history of madness in Marlow's family. During a meeting with his aunt before he finally leaves, Marlow hears more about glory and being "an emissary of light" and "weaning those ignorant millions from their horrid ways." His awkward hint to her that the Company is not embarked on a noble enterprise, but a mercenary one, is brushed aside. Further characterizations of the Company's mission inaugurate Marlow into the "high and just proceedings" of colonialism. He departs Europe on a French steamer that, sailing along the coast of Africa, at one point delivers mail to a man-of-war, "incomprehensibl[y], firing into a continent," at a supposed "enemy" camp of natives. Arriving at his first camp, he is met by six black men chained together, "raw matter" behind which "one of the reclaimed, the product of the new forces at work, strolled despondently."

Integral in and indicative of Marlow's ensuing internal transitions is a slight shift from common perspectives of light and dark. Sunshine in this land is more than once portrayed as "blinding"; light has become a destructive element. To escape from the sun and the silent accusation of the chained black men, Marlow steps into the shade of some trees and discovers a mass of black shapes, the concentrates of human misery wrung out by the "philanthropic" work going on: "pain, abandonment and despair, . . . disease and starvation." As he hastens away, Marlow encounters the white-clad vision of the company's chief accountant, from whom he will initially hear the name of Kurtz. The accountant is the first in a series of personages as thin as their appearances. The accountant's appearance, likened to that of "a hairdresser's dummy," is marked by Marlow to give no indication of the "great demoralization of the land" around him.

Ten days later a caravan arrives, and with it, Marlow departs for Central Station. His only white traveling companion is "rather too fleshy," constantly faints and eventually contracts a fever, which inspires no sympathy in Marlow, but annoyance to the point that he asks the man what he is doing there at all. This unconscious partiality toward survival of nature's physically fittest is the first sign of Marlow's ultimate compliance with the "efficiency" of social Darwinism, the survival of the socially fittest, and the "redeeming idea" behind his entire experience. He eventually arrives at Central Station, only to discover that the steamer of which he is supposedly skipper sunk a few days ago. A mustached man apparently reassures him by insisting, "Everybody had behaved splendidly." Meeting the manager, Marlow remarks that such an ordinary man must have achieved and maintained his position merely by never getting ill. Affirming that "men who come out here should have no entrails," the manager also equates himself with the accountant as one of Joseph Conrad's "hollow men." Marlow's speculation that "perhaps there was nothing within him" refers more to the manager's moral emptiness than to his physical superiority. Frustrated and mildly disgusted, Marlow sets to work rescuing his steamboat. Trying to separate himself from those colonialists whose worship of the ivory idol is no more "glorious" than the Romans' manifestation of brute strength, he rejects the affected reality of the station and finds in work, which those at the station only see as mere show, the opportunity to discover himself and his own reality.

After a fire at Central Station, during which the mustached man is heard again to comment that "everyone is behaving splendidly" as he rushes around filling a leaking pail with water, Marlow meets the manager's assistant, whom he overhears ominously mentioning Kurtz. This "papier-mâché Mephistopheles. . . [with] nothing inside but a little loose dirt," whose function for the past year has supposedly been to make bricks, although there is no sign of bricks in Central Station, supplies Marlow with more details of Kurtz, the chief of the Inner Station: "He is an emissary of pity, and science, and progress . . . higher intelligence, wide sympathies, a singleness of purpose." This resemblance to Marlow's role as an "emissary of light" offers him something he can morally respect, someone perhaps akin to himself; however, this psychological affinity anticipates that Kurtz's moral corruption will precede Marlow's own final compromise of ideals. As the manager's assistant drones on, Marlow marvels at "the silence of the land, the amazing reality of its concealed life," so bluntly in contrast with the unreality surrounding Marlow, "the philanthropic pretense of the whole concern, . . . their talk, . . . their government, . . . their show of work."

Avowing that he detests lies, he then confesses to misleading the manager's assistant regarding his own personal connections. To justify himself, Marlow briefly appeals to the listeners on the *Nellie* to believe that his concealment was to protect his hopes for Kurtz. At this time, the original narrator mentions how in the dark of the night, Marlow has become no more than a voice, just as Kurtz is no more than a word for Marlow. Also, in order to sustain his own moral composure, Marlow begins to revise reality and tells what could be construed as a lie to his foreman about forthcoming rivets. Instead of rivets, however, the manager's uncle arrives with a band of ivory hunters, calling themselves the Eldorado Exploring Expedition.

Part 2 begins with a conversation to which Marlow is unwittingly privy between the manager and his uncle. The manager's career has been threatened by Kurtz; the manager himself even more so because he does not understand the man who sent them boatloads of ivory and then went back to his station; Marlow supposes it is because Kurtz is dedicated to his work.

Soon afterward, the Expedition leaves and is said to have been swallowed up by the wilderness, which Marlow interprets as the insignificance of men in comparison to "the silent wilderness surrounding this cleared speck on earth, waiting patiently for the passing away of this fantastic invasion."

His steamboat finally repaired, Marlow begins his journey to the Inner Station. He comments that the concentration he devotes to making sure his steamboat does not get sunk causes reality to fade, a peculiar statement that seems a modification of Marlow's previous definition of reality. This alteration in his reality becomes more and more evident as he penetrates "deeper and deeper into the heart of darkness." He fancies that he and his crew are "the first of men taking possession of an accursed inheritance, to be subdued at the cost of profound anguish and of excessive toil." Colonialists, like Roman imperialists, are the first men who must face and subdue the wilderness, and Marlow admits that they "are accustomed to look upon the shackled form of a conquered monster, but there—there you could look at a thing monstrous and free." Yet even here, Marlow can look into the face of the men who "howled and leaped, and spun," and find that they too share humanity in common with him. Delving beneath the surface of education and façade, the man who has been made by civilization will encounter the primeval man. The savage who acts as his fireman is still, solely, a savage at heart, dressed up in civilized clothes, unconscious of a self separate from the consciousness of the encompassing wilderness. However, although Marlow enters the wilderness and acknowledges this bestial self, he is conscious of another self, his civilized self, which seems to define his "reality."

About fifty miles below the Inner Station, they come across a hut with some firewood, a note, and a book, *An Inquiry into Some Points of Seamanship,* notated with what Marlow assumes to be cipher. Both he and the manager, superciliously nationalistic, assume the previous visitor to have been English. While they are detained further down the river on the third morning by a "white fog, . . . as blinding as the night," an anguished, tribal cry is emitted from the jungle. As Marlow surveys the "painfully shocked" expression of his white crew and the "essentially quiet" expression of his black crew while waiting for an attack, he wonders that the greater number of cannibals have not preyed on the lesser number of whites and notes the shared trait of restraint in human beings, whether it be the "inborn strength to fight hunger properly" or the manager's desire to "preserve appearances." They are not attacked before the fog lifts, and they continue on. Marlow adopts the impressionistic style of subjective (rather than objective) delineation to describe their approach toward what is first perceived to be an obstructing islet, then a sandbank, and then a series of "shallow patches." Unsuccessfully judging the shoal, Marlow chooses the wrong passage. Consequently, he must steer close to the bank, where they are attacked. In another impressionistic description, the panicked men aboard the steamboat respond to the "little sticks," which turn out to be arrows, by opening fire and squirting lead into the bushes, reminiscent of the man-of-war shooting at the unseen "enemy." The bush howls, Marlow pulls on the steam whistle, and the attackers, frightened away, retreat. Marlow is struck by the idea that Kurtz is dead and says, disappointedly, that now he will never hear Kurtz speak: "The point was in his being a gifted creature, and that of all his gifts the one that stood out pre-eminently, that carried with it a sense of real presence, was his ability to talk." Marlow seems to have lost interest in substance; what matters is no longer Kurtz's ideas, but how he would have expressed himself, the voice having comprised the man. Admitting to the group on the *Nellie* that Kurtz was not dead, however, he launches into a vehement diatribe against the basis of moral failure, the conceit of the individual in society. The insignificance of men compared to the wilderness is complemented by their insignificance as individuals in regard to their own society, wherein they function only as negligible toilers in the contest for survival between the greater collective of society and nature: "your strength comes in . . . your power of devotion, not to yourself, but to an obscure, back-breaking business." Man's perception of himself in relation to the world is impairingly subjective. Although Marlow has assumed that his moral self defined the moral world, he now realizes that it has been the constraints of society that have defined his moral reality, not his own self. He says of Kurtz as well: "All Europe contributed to the making of Kurtz." Thus, the International Society for the Suppression of Savage Customs subsequently employs Kurtz to write a report about the superiority of the white man to the savage man, executed eloquently except for an unrestrained postscript written in at the bottom: "Exterminate all the brutes!" For the sake of the bond of human kinship that he briefly felt with his helmsman, a man from the wilderness, killed during the attack, Marlow protects the body from further exploitation and tips it unceremoniously over the side of the steamboat; his civilized companions are outraged by this display of heartlessness; the accompanying cannibals are outraged because good food has been forfeited.

They are on the verge of turning back when Marlow spots the Inner Station, where they are cheerfully welcomed by a patchwork-outfitted man who tells them that everything is all right, that the attack was all right (recalling the mustached man at the Central Station and implying that, for all the talk of Kurtz's distinction, the situation is no different here). While the manager and some men go on land to fetch Kurtz, Marlow is left with the harlequin, who explains himself to be a young Russian adventurer and the one who left them wood and the note at the hut. Marlow returns the book to him and is informed that what he thought was cipher are notes in Russian. A very surprised Marlow is struck by the youth's inexplicable existence. "His very existence was improbable" (Marlow declares at the beginning of **Part 3**) because he was neither guided by the principles of society (or none that Marlow can understand) nor overcome by the wanton embrace of the wilderness. Lit by the "modest and clear flame" of the "absolutely pure, uncalculating, unpractical spirit of adventure," he has eluded both the darkness of the wilderness and the darkness of civilization. Throughout the passages portraying Africa are constant references to intense light, like the "blazing sky" Marlow cites here. Light has not metaphorically been what it seems. The darkness within this land has been concealed by "blinding sunlight" and "blazing sky," somewhat like the white of the white men, which has concealed the darkness within them.

The knobs of wood on the stakes surrounding Kurtz's house are impressionistically disclosed to be shriveled heads and corroborate Marlow's statement regarding the necessity of social constraints on a civilized man: "They only showed that Mr. Kurtz lacked restraint in the gratification of his various lusts." As Marlow discovered the deficiency within himself, Kurtz, before him, discovered that "the great solitude . . . echoed loudly within him because he was hollow at the core." Although shrouded by a magnificent eloquence, Kurtz too is only as ephemeral as his words, a manufactured product of the civilized world. With this revelation, Marlow notices that "the ruined hovel, beyond the symbolic row of stakes" is in the gloom whilst he and his steamer "were yet in the sunshine."

Kurtz is carried on board. On shore, a "wild and gorgeous apparition of a woman," representing the wilderness that had seduced Kurtz, gestures a flamboyant farewell to the boat and "like the wilderness," regards them with "an air of brooding over an inscrutable purpose," recalling the "gloom brooding over a crowd of men." On board the steamboat, the manager gleefully decries an unsound Kurtz. As he once turned his back on the station, Marlow turns away from the manager, to Kurtz, and then corrects himself to say that he really had turned to the wilderness; but there it is no better: he feels "an intolerable weight, . . . the smell of the damp earth, the unseen presence of victorious corruption." Darkness is everywhere.

Speaking with the harlequin, Marlow advises him to continue as he is, adventuring, assuring the man that "Mr. Kurtz's reputation is safe with me," but uncertain as to how truthful he is being; Marlow is preparing to return to the world of civilization and realizes that appearances must be maintained. During the night, woken by some yelling amidst a beating of drums from the jungle, he checks on Kurtz in his cabin and receives a moral shock, "as if something altogether monstrous, intolerable to thought and odious to the soul, had been thrust upon me." Kurtz, whom he has lied for, once representative to him of civilization's potential, has gone to the wilderness. He does not, however, betray Kurtz; for, "it was ordered I should never betray him—it was written I should be loyal to the nightmare of my choice. I was anxious to deal with this shadow by myself alone." On the bank, he comes upon Kurtz and with restrained desperation says, "You will be lost." Then he unabashedly lies to Kurtz, saying that his reputation has been made and his success in Europe is assured, in order to convince him to return to the boat. Kurtz returns to the boat, and they set back up the river. Finally, the wilderness seems to have bowed its head and seems to watch over the steamboat, "this grimy fragment of another world, the forerunner of change, of conquest, of trade, of massacres, of blessings." Marlow watches over Kurtz; for the temptations of the wilderness and of civilization continue to struggle with Kurtz "for the possession of that soul." He witnesses "the inconceivable mystery of a soul that knew no restraint, no faith, and no fear, yet struggling blindly with itself." The boat breaks down, and some night afterward, from Kurtz's deathbed, his last words confer the final, despairing assertion that the darkness is truly everywhere, filling even oneself: "No eloquence could have been so withering to one's belief in mankind as his final burst of sincerity 'The horror, the horror.'" Broken in spirit, Marlow collapses in fever on his return to England. There he is accosted by the seekers of Kurtz's glorious posterity. Over and over, he lies about Kurtz and suppresses the postscript at the end of the publication for the Society in order to maintain the image that had once been the man. His final lie is to Kurtz's Intended, who asks Marlow what Kurtz's last words had been. He replies that they were her name.

"The Secret Sharer" opens with the narrator and his ship anchored at the head of the Gulf of Siam. He has just taken command as captain for the first time on a ship with which he is unfamiliar. Naively, he expects his crew to be all that they should be, and yet he wonders if he himself will be all that he expects. "I wondered how far I should turn out faithful to that ideal conception of one's own personality every man sets up for himself secretly." Over supper, the young captain, his chief, and his second mates discuss a ship anchored inside the islands, the Liverpool ship *Sephora*. Anxious that the crew has worked hard the last two days without much compensating sleep and restively sleepless himself, the captain astonishes the mate as he prepares to take the anchor watch by taking the watch himself, "an unheard of caprice." Trying to get to know his ship and feel comfortable with it, he strolls about and discovers, irritatingly, that the side ladder has been irresponsibly left in the water. Realizing that he himself had prevented things from being properly taken care of by prematurely dismissing his officers to bed, he attempts to haul the ladder in by himself and is met by startling resistance. Looking overboard, he is met by the horrifying vision of a headless corpse. It turns out to be a black-haired swimmer hanging onto the ladder. The man, who seems to have "risen from the bottom of the sea," asks for the captain, whom the narrator declares himself to be. The captain feels an affinity toward his nocturnal visitor, whom he intuits to be young like himself, an affinity that seems reciprocated when the man comes aboard. An inconspicuous statement here also informs the reader that the narrative is about an experience long past. The captain dresses his visitor in a sleeping suit identical to the one he himself is wearing, and as the captain and his "double" stroll the deck together, the man, Leggatt, confesses to have been the mate of the *Sephora* and to have killed a man, one of his crew, an insurgent who provoked him during the frenzy of a tumultuous storm. During this appeal, the assumption of the confessor as if their "experiences had been as identical" as their sleeping suits, and afterward, when the captain refers again to his "double," the formation of some sort of psychological bond between the two is obvious.

The captain puts his double in his stateroom and alerts the second mate so as to be relieved by him. Returning to his cabin and reassessing the fugitive, he states that "He was not a bit like me, really; yet, . . . we stood . . . whispering side by side, . . . the uncanny sight of a double captain busy talking in whispers with his other self." The psychological allusion is unmistakable, and briefly it is unclear whether the overanxious captain is imagining the man or whether he is real. Continuing his story, Leggatt recounts how he was put under lock and key for killing the man and how he petitioned the skipper to give him a chance of escape, since it was he who had saved the ship during the storm. The skipper refused, but three weeks afterward they arrived at the gulf, and after giving Leggatt his dinner that night, the steward by chance left his door unlocked. Walking about on deck, he had been seized by the urge to jump, and jump over he did. Being a strong swimmer, he had planned to reach a nearby island, but reached the ship instead. The captain realizes that since he is a stranger to the ship, the others could easily suspect him of harboring the fugitive. The psychological imagery in the narrative becomes more profuse as he puts his "other self" to sleep, cannot fall asleep himself due to the "confused sensation of being in two places at once," and is "greatly bothered by an exasperating knocking in my head." Fortunately, the knocking turns out to be his steward bringing him his morning coffee after he has fallen asleep unawares. Having been abruptly awoken and startled again by his steward's sudden reappearance to take away his cup, the young captain becomes extremely uneasy and anxious, which is noticed by his steward, who mentions it to his two officers. The subsequent sneering air of his second mate makes the captain feel a need to assert himself, which he successfully does; but during breakfast with his officers in his cabin, he admits: "the dual working of my mind, . . . constantly watching myself, my secret self, as dependent on my actions as my own personality sleeping in that bed," is maddeningly distracting.

At the beginning of **Part 2** the captain is visited by the skipper of the *Sephora,* and while they are in his cabin together, he feigns deafness in order that the skipper speak louder and his double can share everything. The skipper informs him of the happenings on the *Sephora.* In the course of their conversation, the skipper's fifteen years of experience with the *Sephora* seems equated with his obstinate, merciless adherence to the law, in contrast to the new captain, whose own strong moral convictions seem to have caused him to disregard set standards of conduct. The skipper insinuates that the young captain would not have made a good mate for the *Sephora* either, and in this way "suggested a mysterious similitude to the young fellow he had distrusted and disliked from the first." The remarks about the distance from the *Sephora* to the nearest land and its proximity to the young captain's boat betoken a definite suspicion on the part of the skipper; however, the captain adroitly insists on showing the skipper around his cabin and stateroom, and then the rest of his ship.

The skipper disposed of, the young captain must now continue the show for his own crew. A discussion with his mate leaves him wondering how well he is doing, but he rationalizes it and justifies himself by saying that "it was most trying to be on deck . . . on the whole I felt less torn in two when I was with him [the secret sharer of my cabin]." Still secure, his visitor tells him when they are alone again that contrary to what the skipper reported, the order for the saving foresail was never given and that it was the fugitive who had saved the ship. The captain's conviction is completely apparent when he sums the situation up as having been "The same strung-up force which had given twenty-four men a chance, at least, for their lives, had, in a sort of recoil, crushed an unworthy mutinous existence." After this judgment, he is informed that a wind has risen. His position as captain is now to be tested and he goes on deck "to make the acquaintance of his ship." The presence of "the stranger in his cabin" both aids and hinders him. On the one hand, he states that he is not alone with his command; on the other hand, his actions on deck noticeably reflect his preoccupation with secrecy and stealth, and he says "it's to no commander's advantage to be suspected of ludicrous eccentricities." It is interesting to note that the captain continually portrays himself as uncertain and seems to derive strength from his absconding self, who "looked always perfectly self-controlled, more than calm—almost invulnerable." Yet it is the double who actually relies upon the captain.

The captain continues to harbor his counterpart without suspicion, although his officers definitely think him to be peculiar. One day, however, there is a harrowing incident wherein his steward goes into his bathroom, where the fugitive has been so successfully ensconced, to hang up a coat the captain has left out to dry. The incident passes without a discovery, but the captain shakily returns to his cabin, beginning to doubt his own sanity and the corporeal reality of his double. After this scare, his double concludes that he must be marooned on a nearby island as soon as possible and expresses his appreciation of the bond between them: "I know that you understand. . . . You seem to have been there on purpose. . . . It's very wonderful." The captain hesitates from agreeing to the solution but eventually relents. The next day, he heads for some islands, and after informing his double that he will try to get as close as he can to an island they guess to be Koh-ring, gives an inexplicable order to open the quarter-deck ports. His second mate wonders at this bizarre caprice, and his chief mate glances at him, as if looking for signs of lunacy or drunkenness. The captain informs his secret sharer of the details of his plan and counsels escape. There is a profound farewell, and the plan is activated. In order to allow for the escape, the captain must bring his ship perilously close to the shore. In the ensuing, suspenseful trial of his command, the presence of his second self both physically and mentally vanishes, and the ship is saved by a hat he gave to his second self, which has been left behind on the water during his escape: "It had been meant to save his homeless head from the dangers of the sun. And now—behold—it was saving the ship, by serving me for a mark to help out the ignorance of my strangeness." Finally, unburdened of his second self, he feels "the perfect communion of a seaman with his first command." ✤

—*Sandra Liu*

List of Characters

Charlie Marlow is the protagonist and dominating narrator in *Heart of Darkness.* He delivers his entire narrative on the *Nellie* sitting in a Buddha-like posture, implying enlightenment or perpetual meditation. Naturally curious, idealistically judgmental, and rather too naively self-assured, Marlow joins "the trading society" as a steamboat skipper. His journey down the river and into the interior of the jungle symbolizes the internal exploration of his own moral integrity. Kurtz, with whom Marlow almost immediately identifies, and who is the supposed embodiment of his moral ideals, awaits him at the heart of darkness. Marlow's refusal to lie represents his own ethical integrity: "You know I hate, detest, and can't bear a lie, not because I am straighter than the rest of us, but simply because it appalls me"; yet, as he proceeds from one station to the next and up the river, gradually beginning to internalize the disenchanting corruption of his surroundings, of the redeeming idea of the company and of the wilderness, he draws closer and closer to telling lies. The confrontation with Kurtz marks Marlow's final debilitating recognition of the inadequacy of his personal morals to influence or command circumstances beyond his comprehension and control. Thereafter, it becomes easier and easier for him to lie.

Kurtz's presence in most of *Heart of Darkness* is primarily through the words of other people—a fitting characterization, since his person turns out to be barely more tangible than his voice. The fact that he is half-English and half-French encourages the denigrating ideas about his character that the manager, an Englishman, conceives. He is the chief of the Inner Station and is described as magnetically charming with an incredible faculty for articulated expression. Although he is childishly selfish, materialistic, deluded, and quite mad when Marlow meets him, Conrad infers that he was once a principled man of substance, driven to the wilderness by his ambition to fulfill "immense plans." In the end, he seems to regain himself, dying in a "supreme moment of complete knowledge" and moral possession of his soul.

The narrator of "The Secret Sharer" is unnamed and introduces himself only as a neophyte captain. He is obviously young and insecure regarding his abilities. However, his first action, to take the anchor watch and dismiss his crew and officers to bed, seems guided by promising personal standards. Although he begins somewhat tentatively and definitely self-consciously, as the narrative progresses he will feel more at ease in assuming responsibility. He is justifiably nervous and seems incapable of concealing his anxiety from his crew. Consequently, he lacks any heartening respect from his crew, and his feeling of estrangement from them and his ship persists for most of the narrative. Although he is inspired by the self-assurance of Leggatt, he is also hampered by the ordeal of feeling like a split personality. In the end, when he is unburdened of Leggatt, whose concealment was the result of the captain's youthful brashness and pride, he also finally lets go of his self-effacing doubts and comes into his full right of command.

Leggatt in "The Secret Sharer" functions primarily as the symbolic alter ego of the insecure captain. He is the chief mate of the *Sephora* until a fit of fury and frustration causes him to kill a mutinous subordinate. Strong, both physically and mentally, he escapes cabin arrest on the *Sephora* and swims to the captain's ship. There, he demonstrates himself to be unruffled and composed, certain of his moral virtue regardless of having killed a man. Although he seems more experienced and mature than the captain, his youthfulness is betrayed by his conspicuous pride and compellingly passionate and unaffected earnestness. He seems to survive on inordinate luck and resourcefulness, and also serves as an exemplar of self-assurance and poise for the nervous and uncertain captain. ✤

Critical Views

EDWARD GARNETT ON THE PSYCHOLOGICAL POWER OF *HEART OF DARKNESS*

[Edward Garnett (1868–1937), a noted British critic and editor, wrote many critical works, including *Tolstoy: His Life and Writings* (1914), *Turgenev: A Study* (1917), and *Friday Nights: Literary Criticisms and Appreciations* (1922). In this review of *Youth: A Narrative and Two Other Stories,* Garnett recognizes the psychological power of *Heart of Darkness* in its depiction of the relations between white and black people in Africa.]

"Heart of Darkness," to present its theme bluntly, is an impression, taken from life, of the conquest by the European whites of a certain portion of Africa, an impression in particular of the civilising methods of a certain great European Trading Company face to face with the "nigger." We say this much because the English reader likes to know where he is going before he takes art seriously, and we add that he will find the human life, black and white, in "Heart of Darkness" an uncommonly and uncannily serious affair. If the ordinary reader, however, insists on taking the subject of a tale very seriously, the artist takes his method of presentation more seriously still, and rightly so. For the art of "Heart of Darkness"—as in every psychological masterpiece—lies in the relation of the things of the spirit to the things of the flesh, of the invisible life to the visible, of the sub-conscious life within us, our obscure motives and instincts, to our conscious actions, feelings and outlook. Just as landscape art implies the artist catching the exact relation of a tree to the earth from which it springs, and of the earth to the sky, so the art of "Heart of Darkness" implies the catching of infinite shades of the white man's uneasy, disconcerted, and fantastic relations with the exploited barbarism of Africa; it implies the acutest analysis of the deterioration of the white man's *morale,* when he is let loose from European restraint, and planted down in the tropics as an "emissary of light" armed to the teeth, to make trade profits out of the "subject races." The weirdness, the brilliance, the psychological truth of this masterly analysis of two Continents in conflict, of the abysmal gulf between the white man's system and the black man's comprehension of its results, is conveyed in a rapidly rushing narrative which calls for close attention on the reader's part. But the attention once surrendered, the pages of the narrative are as enthralling as the pages of Dostoyevsky's *Crime and Punishment.* The stillness of the sombre African forests, the glare of the sunshine, the feeling of dawn, of noon, of night on the tropical rivers, the isolation of the unnerved, degenerating whites staring all day and every day at the Heart of Darkness which is alike meaningless and threatening to their own creed and conceptions of life, the helpless bewilderment of the unhappy savages in the grasp of their flabby and rapacious conquerors—all this is a page torn from the life of the Dark Continent—a page which has been hitherto carefully blurred and kept away from European eyes. There is no "intention" in the story, no *parti pris,* no prejudice one way or the other; it is simply a piece of art, fascinating and remorseless, and the artist is but intent on presenting his sensations in that sequence and arrangement whereby the meaning or the meaninglessness of the white man in uncivilised Africa can be felt in its really significant aspects.

—Edward Garnett, "Mr. Conrad's New Book," *Academy and Literature,* 6 December 1902, p. 606

JOSEPH CONRAD ON MARLOW

[Between 1917 and 1920 Joseph Conrad wrote prefaces to his major works for the Uniform Edition of his *Collected Works* (1923–38). In this extract from his introduction to *Youth,* Conrad ponders on the creation of his narrator Marlow and also notes that parts of *Heart of Darkness* derives from his own experiences in Africa.]

'Youth' was not my first contribution to *Maga* ⟨*Blackwood's Edinburgh Magazine*⟩. It was the second. But that story marks the first appearance in the world of the man Marlow, with whom my relations have grown very intimate in the course of years. The origins of that gentleman (nobody as far as I know had ever hinted that he was anything but that)—his origins have been the subject of some literary speculation of, I am glad to say, a friendly nature.

One would think that I am the proper person to throw a light on the matter; but in truth I find that it isn't so easy. It is pleasant to remember that nobody had charged him with fraudulent purposes or looked down on him as a charlatan; but apart from that he was supposed to be all sorts of things; a clever screen, a mere device, a 'personator,' a familiar spirit, a whispering 'daemon.' I myself have been suspected of a meditated plan for his capture.

That is not so. I made no plans. The man Marlow and I came together in the casual manner of those health-resort acquaintances which sometimes ripen into friendships. This one has ripened. For all his assertiveness in matters of opinion he is not an intrusive person. He haunts my hours of solitude, when, in silence, we lay our heads together in great comfort and harmony; but as we part at the end of a tale I am never sure that it may not be for the last time. Yet I don't think that either of us would care much to survive the other. In his case, at any rate, his occupation would be gone and he would suffer from that extinction, because I suspect him of some vanity. I don't mean vanity in the Solomonian sense. Of all my people he's the one that has never been a vexation to my spirit. A most discreet, understanding man. . . . ⟨. . .⟩

Heart of Darkness also received a certain amount of notice from the first; and of its origins this much may be said: it is well known that curious men go prying into all sorts of places (where they have no business) and come out of them with all kinds of spoil. This story, and one other, not in this volume, are all the spoil I brought out from the centre of Africa, where, really, I had no sort of business. More ambitious in its scope and longer in the telling, *Heart of Darkness* is quite as authentic in fundamentals as 'Youth.' It is, obviously, written in another mood, I won't characterize the mood precisely, but anybody can see that it is anything but the mood of wistful regret, of reminiscent tenderness.

—Joseph Conrad, Introduction to *Youth* (1917), *Conrad's Prefaces to His Works* (London: J. M. Dent & Sons, 1937), pp. 71–73

✤

G. Jean-Aubry on the Origin of Kurtz

[Georges Jean-Aubry (1882–1949) was a noted French critic who compiled *Joseph Conrad: Life and Letters* (1927) and wrote *Vie de Conrad* (1947), translated as *The Sea-Dreamer: A Definitive Biography of Joseph Conrad* (1957). In this extract, Jean-Aubry speculates on the possible origin of the figure of Kurtz in *Heart of Darkness.*]

The accuracy of the smallest details (I cite only a few here) related by Marlow in "Heart of Darkness" and their agreement with facts recorded either on the geographical charts or in the Belgian reviews of the period, could not fail to inspire the wish to discover whether the principal character of the story—he who, with the landscape, shapes its very life and soul—is only an invention of Conrad's imagination or a more or less graphic reproduction of an actual human being.

Granted the support of a true life story on which Conrad has most frequently founded his romantic creations, it may well be supposed that in a tale which he himself has declared to be the outcome of experience, the principal character would not be purely and simply a product of the imagination. The name of the character Kurtz seems to me a most singular fact in this connection. Why should Conrad have chosen a name of German consonance in a place where, according to the statistics of the "Bulletin Officiel de l'Etat du Congo", Germans were extremely rare at that time? There were to be found in the Congo Belgians, Frenchmen, Englishmen, and Americans (the latter mostly missionaries), and Scandinavians who were engaged in all kinds of occupations connected with the command, construction, and repair of small vessels navigating the high rivers. The significance of this name is rendered still more evident by the fact that Conrad says in "Heart of Darkness":

> The original Kurtz had been educated partly in England, and, as he was good enough to say himself,—his sympathies were in the right place. His mother was half English, his father was half French. All Europe contributed to the making of Kurtz.

Since these details are of no importance to the story, they would appear to be related with this precision only because they are actual facts. Besides, in the course of a careful study of the works of Conrad, I have observed that when the novelist's characters correspond exactly to persons who have really existed, they retain their real names. In certain cases also, Conrad introduces into his stories a character he has known, who has not indeed played the part attributed to him but who would have been *capable of playing it;* and in this case he retains not only the character and appearance of the person concerned, but also his name. Thus in the course of a conversation I had last year with Captain James Craig—formerly in command of the S.S. *Vidar* on board which, in the capacity of second mate, Joseph Conrad met with the protagonists of *Almayer's Folly*—I learned that nearly all the characters and names in the novel were in exact conformity with truth. Furthermore, in "Youth" Conrad has retained in the officers of the S.S. *Judea* the appearance and names—Beard and Mahon—of the officers of the S.S. "Palestine" on board which, in 1881, he had the experience related in "Youth". Thus, too, in the story of the *Typhoon* he has given to the Captain the name and appearance of Captain McWhirr who in 1887 had been his captain on board the *Highland Forest.* Captain McWhirr, it is true, did not go through the experience related by Conrad in *Typhoon,* but *he would have been capable of acting in the same manner* under similar circumstances. This is true not only of the principal, but also of the more incidental, characters in Conrad's books. Thus in "Youth" he alludes to a shipowner who he says was called Wilmer or Wilcox or something of the kind; the name, in effect, was Wilson. I could give numerous instances of this kind which lead me to believe that if Kurtz was not the name of the actual character it was a near approach to the real name. Investigation of the *Bulletin Officiel de l'Etat du*

Congo for the year 1890 provided me with the following information:

> M. Cloetens has taken over the management of the Kinchassa establishment; M. Gosse that of Matadi, M. Engeringh that of Louebo; M. Mitchells that of the Equator, and M. Klein that of the Falls.

Remember that Marlow said he met with Kurtz at Stanley Falls, the extreme point of navigation of the Congo, and note furthermore his ironical remark on the same character: "Kurtz—Kurtz—that means 'short' in German,—don't it? Well, the name was as true as everything in his life—and death. He looked at least seven feet long." We shall find that the name Klein applies equally to this passage and may be used with the same irony as that of Kurtz. Marlow describes the death of Kurtz on board the same steamer that he commanded. I was curious to know if Klein died in the year 1890. Strange to say, the various Belgian reviews which I read attentively make no mention of it. Mortality, it is true, was high in the Congo at that time and it was not considered desirable to draw too much attention to deaths among officials and merchants living in the Belgian colony. It would have damped the ardor of those desiring to civilize that country described by Stanley as the "Dark Continent". Since the newspapers gave me no enlightenment on the subject of Kurtz, I applied to the Société du Haut-Congo and obtained from them the following record:

> Klein, Georges Antoine, French. Engaged as commercial agent. Left for the Congo the 23rd December 1888. Died on the 21st September as a result of dysentery on board the steamer "Roi des Belges" during a voyage in 1890. Interred in Chumbiri (Bolobo).

It would be impossible without actual proof to judge of the resemblance between Kurtz and Klein; but the presence of Klein on board the S.S. *Roi des Belges* and his death on board that vessel correspond exactly with the dates of the only voyage made by Conrad as its captain; he therefore undoubtedly witnessed the facts related by Marlow. Knowing the psychological procedure of Conrad, we may say with certainty that between the characters Klein the real and Kurtz the fictitious there is more connection than the mere resemblances of names and facts.

—G. Jean-Aubry, "Joseph Conrad in the Heart of Darkness," *Bookman* (New York) 63, No. 4 (June 1926): 433–34

LEONARD F. DEAN ON THE ENDING OF *HEART OF DARKNESS*

[Leonard F. Dean (b. 1909) is a leading critic of Shakespeare who has written *The Play of Language* (1970) and edited *A Casebook on* Othello (1961). In this extract, Dean expresses dissatisfaction with the ending of *Heart of Darkness*.]

The conclusion of "The Heart of Darkness" produces a far different effect, although the intention is the same. The symbolism is melodramatic. The Intended has not earned the quality which she is meant to represent, and her effect is further weakened by the Hollywood set in which she is placed. When she extends her arms, the pose and the calculated manipulation of light, shadow, and black drapery recall too obviously the earlier mechanical symbol of the savage queen on the banks of the Congo. These lapses may be explained in part by reference to limitations in Conrad's artistic resources. The conclusion of the story, unlike the Congo experiences, was probably invented. Conrad's weakness in invention has often been noticed. It is implied by his preoccupation with the importance of reading symbolic meaning into actual experience. A wider explanation, however, is to be reached through a study of his use of Marlow. This fictitious narrator is usually explained as a device for securing aesthetic distance between the reader and the plot, thus reducing the impact of Conrad's romantic material. In "The Heart of Darkness" Marlow does serve to interest us in meaning rather than in brute action, but he also prevents Conrad and the reader from fully experiencing the final tragic effect. It is Marlow rather than Kurtz who returns to affirm his faith in the Intended. This is unsatisfactory because Marlow has only observed Kurtz's horror. His somewhat parallel sickness is an inadequate substitute for Kurtz's complete disillusionment. In fact, Marlow's moral insight appears to be nearly as penetrating at the beginning of his journey as at the end. It was perhaps inevitable, given his artistic function, that he should be a static character.

—Leonard F. Dean, "Tragic Pattern in Conrad's 'The Heart of Darkness,'" *College English* 6, No. 2 (November 1944): 103–4

✤

ALBERT J. GUÉRARD ON THE TRUE FOCUS OF *HEART OF DARKNESS*

[Albert J. Guérard (b. 1914), a former professor of English at Stanford University, is the author of many books, including *Robert Bridges: A Study of Traditionalism in Poetry* (1942), *André Gide* (1951), and *Thomas Hardy* (1964). In this extract from his celebrated study, *Conrad the Novelist* (1958), Guérard argues that *Heart of Darkness* is not about Kurtz or the brutality of European colonialism, but that it is rather about Marlow.]

⟨. . .⟩ it is time to recognize that the story *Heart of Darkness* is not primarily about Kurtz or about the brutality of Belgian officials but about Marlow its narrator. To what extent it also expresses the Joseph Conrad a biographer might conceivably recover, who in 1898 still felt a debt must be paid for his Congo journey and who paid it by the writing of this story, is doubtless an insoluble question. I suspect two facts (of a possible several hundred) are important. First, that going to the Congo was the enactment of a childhood wish associated with the disapproved childhood ambition to go to sea, and that this belated enactment was itself profoundly disapproved, in 1890, by the uncle and guardian. It was another gesture of a man bent on throwing his life away. But even more important may be the guilt of complicity, just such a guilt as many novelists of the Second World War have been obliged to work off. What

Conrad thought of the expedition of the Katanga Company of 1890–1892 is accurately reflected in his remarks on the "Eldorado Exploring Expedition" of "Heart of Darkness": "It was reckless without hardihood, greedy without audacity, and cruel without courage . . . with no more moral purpose at the back of it than there is in burglars breaking into a safe." Yet Conrad hoped to obtain command of the expedition's ship even after he had returned from the initiatory voyage dramatized in his novel. Thus the adventurous Conrad and Conrad the moralist may have experienced collision. But the collision, again as with so many novelists of the second war, could well have been deferred and retrospective, not felt intensely at the time.

So much for the elusive Conrad of the biographers and of the "Congo Diary." Substantially and in its central emphasis "Heart of Darkness" concerns Marlow (projection to whatever great or small degree of a more irrecoverable Conrad) and his journey toward and through certain facets or potentialities of self. F. R. Leavis seems to regard him as a narrator only, providing a "specific and concretely realized point of view." But Marlow reiterates often enough that he is recounting a spiritual voyage of self-discovery. He remarks casually but crucially that he did not know himself before setting out, and that he likes work for the chance it provides to "find yourself . . . what no other man can ever know." The Inner Station "was the farthest point of navigation and the culminating point of my experience." At a material and rather superficial level, the journey is through the temptation of atavism. It is a record of "remote kinship" with the "wild and passionate uproar," of a "trace of a response" to it, of a final rejection of the "fascination of the abomination." And why should there not be the trace of a response? "The mind of man is capable of anything—because everything is in it, all the past as well as all the future." Marlow's temptation is made concrete through his exposure to Kurtz, a white man and sometime idealist who had fully responded to the wilderness: a potential and fallen self. "I had turned to the wilderness really, not to Mr. Kurtz." At the climax Marlow follows Kurtz ashore, confounds the beat of the drum with the beating of his heart, goes through the ordeal of looking into Kurtz's "mad soul," and brings him back to the ship. He returns to Europe a changed and more knowing man. Ordinary people are now "intruders whose knowledge of life was to me an irritating pretence, because I felt so sure they could not possibly know the things I knew."

On this literal plane, and when the events are so abstracted from the dream-sensation conveying them, it is hard to take Marlow's plight very seriously. Will he, the busy captain and moralizing narrator, also revert to savagery, go ashore for a howl and a dance, indulge unspeakable lusts? The late Victorian reader (and possibly Conrad himself) could take this more seriously than we; could literally believe not merely in a Kurtz's deterioration through months of solitude but also in the sudden reversions to the "beast" of naturalistic fiction. Insofar as Conrad does want us to take it seriously and literally, we must admit the nominal triumph of a currently accepted but false psychology over his own truer intuitions. But the triumph is only nominal. For the personal narrative is unmistakably authentic, which means that it explores something truer, more fundamental, and distinctly less material: the night journey into the unconscious, and confrontation of an entity within the self. "I flung one shoe overboard, and became aware that that was exactly what I had been looking forward to—a talk with Kurtz." It little matters what, in terms of psychological symbolism, we call this double or say he represents: whether the Freudian id or the Jungian shadow or more vaguely the outlaw. And I am afraid it is impossible to say where Conrad's conscious understanding of his story began and ended. The important thing is that the introspective plunge and powerful dream seem true; and are therefore inevitably moving.

—Albert J. Guérard, *Conrad the Novelist* (Cambridge: Harvard University Press, 1958), pp. 37–39

✤

Frederick R. Karl on the Significance of "The Secret Sharer"

[Frederick R. Karl (b. 1927) is a professor of English at New York University and the author of many books, including *The Contemporary English Novel* (1962) and *An Age of Fiction: The Nineteenth Century British Novel* (1964). In this extract, Karl maintains that the significance of "The Secret Sharer" lies in the self-knowledge and maturity that the captain gains.]

"The Secret Sharer" has been the target of more many-sided interpretations than any other Conrad work with the possible exception of "Heart of Darkness." Rather than repeat the literal, ethical, psychological, and aesthetic meanings of the story, I should prefer to examine "The Secret Sharer" in a context that partakes of all the other possibilities and still remains true to Conrad's work as a whole. "The Secret Sharer" deals principally and simply with the theme of apprenticeship-to-life, which is the same theme of growing up and maturing that Conrad treated in many other stories and novels. Placed in this large category, the story can then be seen, as necessary, in its various subdivisions of ethical, psychological, and aesthetic development.

Excessive emphasis on the psychological phenomenon of the alter ego belabors what is the most obvious and perhaps the weakest part of the story. If Conrad stressed any one thing, he stressed the resemblance, both physically and psychologically, between the Captain and the fugitive Leggatt. The constant parallel descriptions of the two men, the use of doubles, doubling, second self, secret self, other self, and so on, are tedious. The repetition is as evident in this story as Marlow's use of qualifying adjectives in "Heart of Darkness." In both stories, of course, much still remains after we have put the obvious behind us.

"The Secret Sharer" is the other side of *Under Western Eyes:* the Captain is a Razumov who does not betray his trust, and Leggatt is a Haldin who escapes his oppressors. The two works taken together pose a double question and show the consequences leading from both answers: what happens when you betray a trust? and what happens when under duress you remain true to your secret? It is the Captain's recognition of these points that sustains the dramatic interest of the story.

Professor Zabel, in his well-known essay "Joseph Conrad: Chance and Recognition," remarked that the crisis in every one of Conrad's novels and stories arrives when by accident, decision, or error a man finds himself abruptly committed to his destiny. This recognition, Zabel says, occurs through a series of steps: isolation of the character from society; his recognition of his situation in a hostile world; and then, once self-knowledge is attained, his way, as we saw with Razumov, of either solving or succumbing to his problem. This is also the problem of the artist; and Conrad through his particular way of developing "The Secret Sharer" was able to relate the psychological and moral contradictions in human nature to the ambivalence of reality as art embodies it, and finally to a searching analysis of value itself. Commensurate with this search for value in life, another way of looking at "Heart of Darkness" suggests itself (with "The Secret Sharer" also in mind): the journey of Marlow-Conrad into the Congo is a means to self-knowledge in which the crucial experience is a process of maturation into both adulthood and artistry; once the journey into this turmoil of experience has been resolved, the survivor is able to proceed to live and create. The experiences of Marlow-Conrad in the Congo, together with the Captain's experience on his ship, are forms of initiation which all must undergo, but which only the true artist in life or fiction can successfully sustain.

Self-knowledge is as much a key to survival as it is to artistic creation; and self-knowledge is one of the chief ingredients in the apprenticeship novel. Jim's personal tragedy is that he unconsciously continues to romanticize a situation that can be alleviated only by a stancher view of reality, a view impossible, perhaps, for one as self-destructive as Jim. As a "successful" Jim, the Captain in "The Secret Sharer" is faced by the stern materials of his salvation and is courageous enough to act on his problem once he has intuitively formulated its substance. This story, then, becomes a microcosm of Conrad's major themes; but for all its suggestiveness, it is, paradoxically, one of his most straightforward and obvious works. Its narrative is a model of clarity, like those uncomplicated narratives "Youth" and *The Shadow Line* (1917).

In giving the terms of initiation into maturity and/or art, Conrad was traveling very familiar and sure ground; in failing, however, to wrap the story in artistic form, he made every point a stated point and every psychological-ethical commentary a labored verbal explanation. In fact, when Conrad continues to force the obvious physical parallels between the two men, the story often loses its thrust in a welter of amateur behaviorism.

Even R. W. Stallman's interpretation of the story's aesthetic level (according to this view, the story objectified a particular crisis in Conrad's life as an artist, a crisis in which he had to come to final terms with his aims as a creator) is purely speculative, depending as it does on broad critical extension of objective correlatives in the narrative. The scenes and images of "Heart of Darkness," for example, are of a variety which permits extension, and an almost limitless number of references are possible. But "The Secret Sharer" is notable for its lack of variety, for the sameness of its images, for its failure to conceptualize the material in less direct form. This is surely not to denigrate the story, but only to show where analysis is possible and where excessive probing may go wrong. I want to emphasize that even though "The Secret Sharer" does not contain cosmic significance, it is, concerning matters of doctrine as well as intrinsically, among Conrad's more important works. The surface in this case *is* the story, and the surface is the arrival of the Captain at a degree of maturity in which he gains self-respect and confidence. This is the obvious fact of "The Secret Sharer," and it must remain of the greatest import.

—Frederick R. Karl, *A Reader's Guide to Joseph Conrad* (New York: Noonday Press, 1960), pp. 231–34

ROYAL A. GETTMANN AND BRUCE HARKNESS ON THE MORAL QUESTIONS OF "THE SECRET SHARER"

[Royal A. Gettmann (b. 1904) is the editor of The Rime of the Ancient Mariner: *A Handbook* (1961). Bruce Harkness (b. 1923), the Dean of Arts and Sciences at Kent State University, has edited Conrad's *The Secret Agent* (1989). In this extract, Gettmann and Harkness assert that it is the moral aspect of "The Secret Sharer" that most concerned Conrad.]

"The Secret Sharer" is of a class of stories all too rare. It has, as so many modern stories do not, a sustained and combined appeal. It offers the immediate appeal of an action or adventure story as well as the aesthetic pleasures of symbolic, psychological, and moral investigation. Most commentaries on the story, though often excellent, tend to concentrate on the technical beauties of the piece as it presents the theme of the "double" man—the psychological aspect. Although clearly recognizing that the story's symbolism has a moral as well as a psychological content, many critics have fixed their discussion on Conrad's presentation of Leggatt as the Captain's hidden self, his alter ego. This critical concentration has led Marvin Mudrick (in the article reprinted in this volume) to an attack on the critics—and on the story—as a labored and wordy statement that man has an inner self and that the inner self is not so good as it might be.

In the final analysis, Conrad's greatest interest is in the moral aspect of the story. At the level of action he adds little to Lubbock's account; likewise the possible social issues are played down—Conrad, for example, has no reference in civil or maritime law for his conclusion, nor does he bring in the point that the victim, John Francis, was a Negro, which could have been used to give an entirely different and social focus to the story. What Conrad adds to Lubbock are the psychological and the moral elements. And our interest in the psychological should be counterbalanced by an analysis of the story's moral range. What is Conrad saying about moral problems *through* what he is saying about psychological facts? For that seems to us the proper stress of one's reading.

When the Captain states the theme early in the story, saying "I wondered how far I should turn out faithful to that ideal conception of one's own personality every man sets up for himself secretly," he is talking about more than psychology: he is worried about his moral state. That the story is primarily moral is brought out clearly later on in the tale. It is, for example, a matter of *conscience* for the Captain to bring the ship closer into shore than he need for so strong a swimmer as Leggatt.

Guerard implies that the story, insofar as we interpret it according to the Captain-narrator's motives for sheltering

Leggatt, is essentially psychological: "the reasons for the narrator's act are defined as 'psychological (not moral).' " This evidence, however, can be taken to have a very different significance. Guerard is referring to the scene in which Captain Archbold confronts our Captain. "I could not, I think," says the narrator, "have met him by a direct lie, again for psychological (not moral) reasons. If he had only known how afraid I was of his putting my feeling of identity with the other to the test"!

But what Conrad is saying here is that the psychological aspect of the story is *settled;* it is the moral issue that is still operating. "A mysterious communication" exists between Leggatt and the Captain from the first moment they meet. That psychological issue that is resolved long before Archbold arrives, but the moral problem still exists. It is this side of the situation, not the psychological, that gives the shape and drive of the story. In other words, one suspects that Guerard takes the narrator to mean that he had no moral qualms about lying to Archbold, but for psychological reasons he couldn't—and he knew he couldn't—give the direct lie. Perhaps the sentence would bear this meaning, but in context, and as it relates to the plot of the story, the meaning is very nearly the opposite: the psychological problems have been solved, but the moral ones remain and are those which are being struggled with—though often in terms of the psychological. At the very least, the sentence cannot be said to "define" the reasons for the Captain's decision to harbor Leggatt.

We suggest, then, not only that the basic theme of "The Secret Sharer" is a moral one, but that emphasizing this aspect of the story will minimize such questions as Guerard's on the last paragraph of the tale. In his "Direction One" monograph on Conrad, Guerard feels that the ending does violence to the symbolism:

> . . . The story is . . . surely a study of the preconscious and the subconscious. . . . Leggatt is not a fragment of the Captain's imagination but a created symbol. . . . The marked advantages of lucid definition through the body of the story more than compensate for the wrenching of the symbol at the end. Theoretically, Leggatt should have remained on the ship, "locked up" perhaps . . .—unless we argue that once we have faced and conquered our dark potentialities we have conquered

> them for good and all. But to have Leggatt remain in the ship would of course have ruined the first and purely adventurous level of the story.

Guerard, in other words, considers Leggatt as primarily a psychological symbol, and is forced to refer the ending to the level of the adventure story (as well as, earlier, to grant as barely acceptable Gustav Morf's theory that the story is another example of the theme of *Lord Jim:* "paralysis through identification with guilt").

There are at least two responses called for here. First, to question whether all details in the story—or any such story—are equally significant in all its aspects of meaning. For example, is the "young cub" of a second mate equally significant in the adventurous, psychological, and moral strands? Clearly not. Second, to point out that the psychological problem (or error on Conrad's part) which Guerard raises is considerably less significant in the moral reading of the story. It seems to us that only if one takes the tale to be essentially psychological can he interpret the last paragraph as a wrenching of the symbolism of "The Secret Sharer."

> —Royal A. Gettmann and Bruce Harkness, "Morality and Psychology in 'The Secret Sharer,'" *Conrad's "The Secret Sharer" and the Critics,* ed. Bruce Harkness (Belmont, CA: Wadsworth Publishing, 1962), pp. 127–29

✤

EDWARD W. SAID ON THE CAPTAIN IN "THE SECRET SHARER"

[Edward W. Said (b. 1935), a leading literary critic, is Old Dominion Foundation Professor of Humanities at Columbia University. Among his many books are *Orientalism* (1978), *Literature and Society* (1980), and *Culture and Imperialism* (1993). In this extract from his book on Conrad, Said argues that the world of the captain in "The Secret Sharer" is a world of British colonial superiority and arrogance.]

Conrad has now established the sweep of his literary universe: he has question-begged away the process by which truth is corrupted into serviceable ideas by man's egoism. England and her closet of imagery have become his, shielding him from the heart of darkness. And it is precisely into this eminently British realm, inhabited with youthful discomposure by the narrator of "The Secret Sharer," that Conrad introduces Leggatt.

The challenge before the neophyte captain (whom I shall call X) is seen against an English background of "fair play" and innate racial superiority. His ideal conception of himself, he thinks, will have to be tried according to British tradition and the exigencies of Leggatt's difficult, but unmistakably British, presence. X's self-conscious effort to play his part is not only to keep Leggatt safe; he also wants to keep his activity within certain strategic restrictions. Together, the two young men threaten these restrictions by revealing their discontent with them. Leggatt shares X's unadmitted wish to escape from the national, social, and philosophic prison in which for better or for worse X had, like Conrad, willfully placed himself. In order to attain goals that his prison does not allow, X must honestly ask himself the question: Am I able to realize my ideal of freedom by myself? The question is answered when X receives the man out of the dark, as a phosphorescent gleam of light emanating from the indifferent sea, and keeps him hidden on board as a temporary apostle of unrestricted freedom. X performs his risky concealment of the fugitive, but then goes no further. It is difficult to believe, as some critics have suggested, that X is a great deal better for his brief encounter with Leggatt. Leggatt simply increases X's confidence in the world of his previous choice. There is no probing of the idea because that idea "will not stand much looking into." Once X has no more use for Leggatt, Leggatt returns to the sea.

Just as a storm gains its full identity in the heart of the exemplary sailor who resists its attack, so Leggatt's presence on the ship endows X with an image of his secret self. But the image is both covert and strangely shameful. On his own ship, in bondage to its limited world, alienated from his crew, X uses Leggatt to gain an even more determined hold on himself *as he is.* The test of his 'ideal' view of himself returns X to the

British world he knows best. In short, "The Secret Sharer" is a hortatory intellectual fable about why a tricky escape from so-called duty is not after all possible. The image of the double, and with it a plot that tests the hero, does not occasion the searching, profoundly serious self-examination that Marlow, say, undergoes in *Heart of Darkness.* Conrad chose what was certainly the easier treatment of the theme, perhaps because—as I have already suggested—by the time of "The Secret Sharer" he had exhausted himself in his own struggles with darkness. By seeing an image of himself in another person, X can ascertain his own identity and exert a tamer, less exacting assault upon his surroundings. When Leggatt swims off to a new destiny, there is a significant absence of further description of X's future. A letter from Conrad to Galsworthy of May 5, 1905, is especially revealing on this point:

> I own I expected good news from you. They are none the less welcome for that. I was more concerned than uneasy at your seediness, which I seemed to know so well. It was like beholding one's own weird acquaintance in a looking glass: my own well known mysterious, disturbing sensations reflected in your personality, which is as near the inner me as anything not absolutely myself can be. I saw you depart from Naples with a feeling of confidence that no usual current mistrust of life could qualify. You were going off in good hands. And I returned tranquil as to your fate—to the tortures of my awful, overwhelming indolence—the very negation of tranquility—just as a cage is not a shelter, is the negation of a place of rest.

If X is later to suffer like this, from indolence, we can be sure that it will be because he has lived in a cage that looks like a shelter.

—Edward W. Said, *Joseph Conrad and the Fiction of Autobiography* (Cambridge, MA: Harvard University Press, 1966), pp. 156–58

JOHN A. PALMER ON THE CAPTAIN'S RELATIONSHIP WITH LEGGATT IN "THE SECRET SHARER"

[John A. Palmer (1926–1982), formerly a professor of English at Cornell University, is the editor of *Twentieth Century Interpretations of* The Nigger of the "Narcissus" (1969) and the author of *Joseph Conrad's Fiction* (1968), from which the following extract is taken. Here, Palmer explores the dual nature of the captain in "The Secret Sharer" and his relationship with the fugitive Leggatt.]

Once it is seen that the impulse toward identification and communication is shared by the narrator and Leggatt, "The Secret Sharer" becomes a story of integration, rather than conflict and repression. To "subdue" Leggatt would be a mistake (delegated here to the legalistic Captain Archbold of the *Sephora*); the narrator must instead fuse Leggatt's subrational personality with his own rational and civilized one, to emerge as a conceptually imperfect but pragmatically effective and healthy moral agent. It is not that the Captain cannot be commander of his ship until Leggatt has left it, but rather that until he has made his full and active practical commitment to Leggatt—risked everything to guarantee Leggatt's freedom and survival, instead of his repression—he cannot feel the self-assurance and practical force necessary to command either himself or his ship, just as Captain Anthony, in a similar situation, cannot acquire command until he has accepted the force and unruliness of his own passion for Flora. "The Secret Sharer" in a sense dramatizes Stein's paradox; the Captain fuses his dual nature, and in so doing makes the destructive part of himself serve his ideal ends. The process of identification and integration is revealed in the narrator's language, which proceeds in such a way as to draw Leggatt and himself into continuously more intimate relations, until finally at the end they are indistinguishable—a fact which helps resolve the puzzle of the story's last sentence. ⟨. . .⟩

Paralleling this linguistic development is a more obvious dramatic and emotional identification. When he first sees Leggatt in the water, the Captain finds that he wants him to emerge into the light and air: "He made no motion to get out of the water. . . . It was inconceivable that he should not attempt to come on board, and strangely troubling to suspect that perhaps he did not want to. And my first words were prompted by just that troubled incertitude." Leggatt is hidden first in the Captain's cabin, then in bed and bathroom (inviting all amateur Freudians to go to work); and finally, in a significant bit of maritime intimacy, he shares the Captain's bunk. The Captain's sympathy with Leggatt progresses from his first protective impulses, to his generous description of Leggatt's murderous behavior as a mere "fit of temper," to his conflict over whether to lie directly to the Captain of the *Sephora* (he does, of course, lie indirectly), and finally to an explicit recognition that he wishes Leggatt's freedom: "My hesitation in letting that man swim away from my ship's side had been a mere sham sentiment, a sort of cowardice." Their final symbolic union is, significantly, wordless: "Our hands met gropingly, lingered united in a steady, motionless clasp for a second. . . . No word was breathed by either of us when they separated." And in the end, of course, his identification with Leggatt saves the Captain's command. Having rammed his floppy hat onto Leggatt's head to protect him from the sun ("I saw myself wandering barefooted, bareheaded, the sun beating on my dark poll"), the Captain sees it floating on the water after Leggatt has returned to the depths, and is able to save his ship by using it as a navigation point. If the Captain is saved by his impulsive gesture of capping Leggatt with the rationality symbolized in the hat, it is Leggatt's acceptance, and not his repression, that matters. This reading is confirmed finally by one striking detail which simply rules out the notion that Leggatt is "subdued" at the end of the story: the first emphatic gesture of self-determination the Captain makes in the story's final moment of crisis, drifting under the shadow of Koh-ring, is to sublimate the murderous behavior of Leggatt and use it as an instrument of just-barely-legal discipline. Leggatt had held his victim by the throat and shaken him like a rat; the Captain disciplines his fear-ridden chief in the same way:

> I caught his arm as he was raising it to batter his poor devoted head, and shook it violently.
>
> "She's ashore already," he wailed, trying to tear himself away.
>
> "Is she? . . . Keep good full there!"

> "Good full, sir," cried the helmsman in a frightened, thin, childlike voice.
>
> I hadn't let go the mate's arm and went on shaking it. "Ready about, do you hear? You go forward"—shake—"and stop there"—shake—"and hold your noise"—shake—"and see these head-sheets properly overhauled"—shake, shake—shake.

In this fusion of conscience and daring lies the secret of self-determination: the sails are properly raised before the breeze, the ship is filled with "cheery cries," the mate assumes his proper function of giving "various orders," and the Captain feels himself in "perfect communion of a seaman with his first command." The "ideal conception of one's own personality every man sets up for himself secretly," which the narrator had meditated upon at the beginning of the story, is neither the nautical priggishness of Captain Archbold nor the uncontrolled impulse of a Leggatt, but something emerging from their conflict and superseding both.

—John A. Palmer, *Joseph Conrad's Fiction: A Study in Literary Growth* (Ithaca, NY: Cornell University Press, 1968), pp. 225–29

Lawrence Graver on the Role of Archbold in "The Secret Sharer"

[Lawrence Graver (b. 1931) is a professor of English at Williams College. He is the author of *Carson McCullers* (1969) and *Samuel Beckett:* Waiting for Godot (1989). In this extract from *Conrad's Short Fiction* (1969), Graver argues that Archbold is the villain of "The Secret Sharer."]

⟨. . .⟩ Archbold is clearly the villain of "The Secret Sharer." Personally inadequate against the pressure of the storm, he refuses to admit Leggatt's heroic role and retreats to an unthinking reliance on Providence. Instead of responding flexibly to the exceptional circumstances of the murder, he becomes increasingly more rigid and more mystical. Archbold's failure of imagination, his inability to see that the moment called for charity not intransigence, testifies to the correctness and decency of the captain's response. Conrad, often scathing about sentimental benevolence, here gives Leggatt the benefit of every doubt and makes him worthy of pity in a way that a James Wait is not.

When the captain hears Leggatt confirm Archbold's fecklessness, he makes his final judgment of the affair: " 'I quite understand,' I conveyed that sincere assurance into his ear . . . It was all very simple. The same strung-up force which had given twenty-four men a chance at least for their lives, had, in a sort of recoil, crushed an unworthy mutinous existence." His response follows a familiar pattern. After a forceful conversation with Leggatt, he can spare "no leisure to weigh the merits of the matter," but goes out "to make the acquaintance of my ship."

Despite this renewed effort, the captain's self-mastery remains for a time incomplete. Unable to forget Leggatt or the suspicions of his crew, he admits that he requires deliberation to perform acts that for a confident commander would be instinctive. At each new threat of exposure, he becomes increasingly apprehensive, while Leggatt continues "perfectly self-controlled, more than calm—almost invulnerable." When the steward opens the door of the bathroom in which Leggatt is hiding, the captain nearly swoons with terror; and before he learns of Leggatt's safety, he automatically stresses the inexplicable, nightmarish quality of events. But once again, when he learns the mundane truth, he marvels at "something unyielding" in Leggatt's character "which was carrying him through so finely."

Much has been made of the severity of the captain's self-division at this point in the tale, though not enough, I think, of the comic quality of the action. The adventures that throw the Captain into fits of nervous anxiety are hardly sinister. He startles the steward who thought he had been below and then sends him around the ship on incomprehensible errands. How can one speak solemnly about dark nights of the soul when the antic disposition is so reminiscent of *Room Service?*

Following the narrow escape in the bathroom, Leggatt asks to be marooned, and after an initial protest the Captain accepts the challenge. There is no need to probe the unconscious to understand his ambivalent motives: he recognizes the value of getting rid of Leggatt, but is frightened of losing the man who so vividly inspires confidence. Once he accepts the inevitability of Leggatt's departure, the captain begins to conform more closely to the ideal of the perfect commander. Decisiveness becomes a matter of instinct as he fulfills Coleridge's formula for maturity: "act spontaneously, not with reflection; but it is your duty to study, inform yourself, and reflect so that you progressively become the kind of person whose spontaneous reflection is wise." Just before the climactic moment, he gives the fugitive three sovereigns and, on "sudden thought," rams his floppy hat on Leggatt's head to protect him from the sun. To insure Leggatt's safety, and as a gesture of self-assertion, he sails dangerously close to shore. As Leggatt goes over the side, the Captain—with the hat as a marker—executes the daring maneuver which puts him back on course, in "perfect communion" with his first command.

What, then, has Leggatt meant to the captain? Exemplary but not necessary ideal, Leggatt represents a kind of behavior, a physical stance so to speak, which inspires the captain to act boldly himself. Having profited from his presence, the captain is now a better and luckier man than Leggatt, who—despite the declamatory ending—is faced with an uncertain future. The description of the fugitive in the final lines is still another index to the weakness of "The Secret Sharer." To call Leggatt "a free man, a swimmer striking out for a new destiny" is a triumph of grandiloquence over the facts of the case. Whatever one might say about Leggatt's resolution in the past, his future can hardly at this point be cause for celebration. An exile, swimming in the darkness toward an unknown island, his destiny may be new but not exactly enviable. The pretentious romanticism at the close has a revealing analogue in a later Conrad story. When Geoffrey Renouard, in "The Planter of Malata," commits suicide by swimming out to sea, the narrator remarks: "Nothing was ever found—and Renouard's disappearance remained in the main inexplicable. For to whom could it have occurred that a man would set out calmly to swim beyond the confines of life—with a steady stroke—his eyes fixed on a star!" The high-coloring here and in the last line of "The Secret Sharer" recalls "Gaspar Ruiz," not "Heart of Darkness."

Some of the rhetorical embroidery in "The Secret Sharer" is surely temperamental (none of Conrad's major works is wholly free from it); but some is due to the uneasy relationship between Conrad and the magazine audience. The story's excessive length may have been the result of *Harper's* rigid yardstick (it fit neatly into two issues in the summer of 1910); and the three dozen synonyms for "double" seem designed to accentuate a dramatic point for fear of having it missed. Although the repetition reassured readers in 1910, it has proven fatal to critics since then. Because of its insistent promptings and seductive detail, "The Secret Sharer" has become everybody's Rorschach test. But its psychology remains elementary; its finest effects are explicit and traditionally moral.

—Lawrence Graver, *Conrad's Short Fiction* (Berkeley: University of California Press, 1969), pp. 156–58

✤

NORMAN SHERRY ON KURTZ AND MARLOW

[Norman Sherry (b. 1926), a British literary critic, is the Mitchell Distinguished Professor of Literature at Trinity University in San Antonio, Texas. He has written *Conrad's Eastern World* (1966) and *The Life of Graham Greene* (1989). In this extract from *Conrad's Western World* (1971), Sherry examines the character of Kurtz in *Heart of Darkness* and the meeting between Kurtz and Marlow.]

In *Heart of Darkness* the meeting with Kurtz is the central point of tension and meaning: 'I went up that river to . . . where I met the poor chap. It was the farthest point of navigation and the culminating point of my experience.' Gradually, Marlow's purpose of taking a steamboat up-river is transmuted into a search for the man he has heard so much about. Since Georges Antoine Klein was certainly not the inspiration for Kurtz's more sensational qualities, it can be concluded that Marlow's growing interest in Kurtz, to the point where to meet him becomes Marlow's primary aim, cannot reflect an aspect of Conrad's journey. Yet there is a strong sense in the story that, given its autobiographical basis, someone like Kurtz probably existed and somehow was part of the design Conrad saw being woven in the area.

In support of this thesis is the method by which Kurtz is introduced—by means of the gossip of the various characters Marlow encounters. This is, of course, an excellent literary technique which engages and raises the reader's interest, at once creating suspense, plot and a basic irony, but it is also a process of acquaintanceship existing in real life. It is possible, then, that Conrad found the inspiration for Kurtz while he was in the Congo, and therefore that someone approximating to Kurtz was in the area then, someone who was sufficiently noticeable to be talked of in such a way.

If we ignore for the moment Kurtz's final involvement with the powers of darkness, the attributes and characteristics he is allotted are not at all improbable ones in that situation, although it might be felt that, taken together, such qualities add up to an unusual being. For Kurtz is outstanding on many levels—as a commercial agent, as a man of artistic and creative merit, and as a man of lofty moral principles which lift him above the level of the common trader.

Marlow hears of him first as a trader from the company's chief accountant:

> One day he remarked, without lifting his head, 'In the interior you will no doubt meet Mr. Kurtz.' On my asking who Mr. Kurtz was, he said he was a first-class agent; and seeing my disappointment at this information, he added slowly, laying down his pen, 'He is a very remarkable person.' Further questions elicited from him that Mr. Kurtz was at present in charge of a trading post, a very important one, in the true ivory-country, at 'the bottom of there. Sends in as much ivory as all the others put together'.

The manager at the Central Station assures Marlow that 'Mr Kurtz was the best agent they had, an exceptional man, of the greatest importance to the Company'.

It is while Marlow is traveling up-river towards Kurtz and his station that he thinks over his knowledge of Kurtz: 'Hadn't I been told in all the tones of jealousy and admiration that he had collected, bartered, swindled, or stolen more ivory than all the other agents together?' And at the Inner Station there is the huge collection of ivory:

> Ivory? I should think so. Heaps of it, stacks of it. The old mud shanty was bursting with it. You would think there was not a single tusk left either above or below the ground in the whole country. 'Mostly fossil', the manager had remarked, disparagingly. It was no more fossil than I am; but they call it fossil when it is dug up. It appears these niggers do bury the tusks sometimes—but evidently they couldn't bury this parcel deep enough to save the gifted Mr. Kurtz from his fate. We filled the steamboat with it, and had to pile a lot on the deck.

Kurtz, moveover, who is 'remarkable' and 'exceptional', is talked of by everyone, is expected to go far—'Oh, he will go far, very far . . . He will be a somebody in the Administration before long. They, above—the Council in Europe, you know—mean him to be'—and has unusual influence with the Council in Europe: 'He has asked the Administration to be sent there [the Inner Station] with the idea of showing what he could do; and I was instructed accordingly. Look at the influence that man must have. Is it not frightful?'

He is also a man of wide gifts. A painting of his hangs in the brick-maker's hut, and of 'all his gifts the one that stood out pre-eminently, that carried with it a sense of real presence, was his ability to talk, his words—the gift of expression'. Proof of this lies in his report for 'the International Society for the Suppression of Savage Customs': 'It was eloquent, vibrating with eloquence, but too high-strung I think. Seventeen pages of close writing he had found time for.' And when he talked all night to the Harlequin, 'The night did not seem to last an hour'. Moreover, he is an explorer: 'he had discovered lots of villages, a lake too.'

And as if this were not enough, Kurtz is 'an emissary of pity, and science, and progress,' 'a gifted creature', a man of high beliefs and principles, as his report shows:

> But it was a beautiful piece of writing. The opening paragraph, however, in the light of later information, strikes me now as ominous. He began with the argument that we whites, from the point of development we had arrived at, 'must necessarily appear to the [savages] in the nature of supernatural beings—we approach them with the might as of a deity', and so on, and so on. 'By the simple exercise of our will we can exert a power for good practically unbounded', etc. etc. From that point he soared and took me with him. The peroration was magnificent, though difficult to remember, you know. It gave me the notion of an exotic Immensity ruled by an august Benevolence. It made me tingle with enthusiasm.

Kurtz is of 'the new gang—the gang of virtue', as opposed to the common run of agents. He has 'higher intelligence, wider sympathies, a singleness of purpose' which are needed 'for the guidance of the cause intrusted to us by Europe'.

If a man even approximating Kurtz in these attributes existed in the Congo during 1890, Conrad must surely have heard of him. And there was such a man. Klein was, as we know, working under the orders of a much more important agent. This man was Arthur Eugene Constant Hodister, and his character, charisma and success, as I have been able to re-discover them, suggest that he was at least in part the inspiration for Kurtz. Hodister was a highly successful commercial agent and explorer, a man of wide abilities, and a man of principles who was definitely on the side of virtue. He had, moreover, influential friends in Europe, and he did go far in terms of his career.

I do not think that Conrad ever met Hodister, but I believe that he heard of him, through gossip and hearsay, in much the way he records Marlow's hearing of Kurtz and, just as Kurtz became a topic of conversation at the Company Station and then especially at the Central Station, it is very likely that Conrad heard Hodister talked of at Matadi, but that such references to him increased enormously once he reached Kinchassa.

—Norman Sherry, *Conrad's Western World* (Cambridge: Cambridge University Press, 1971), pp. 92–95

✤

C. B. Cox on Kurtz's Native Mistress

[C. B. Cox (b. 1928), a professor of English at the University of Manchester, is the author of *The Free Spirit* (1963) and *Joseph Conrad: The Modern Imagination* (1974), from which the following extract is taken. Here, Cox explores the possible purposes of Conrad's use of Kurtz's native mistress.]

Kurtz's native woman appears to Marlow as a wild and gorgeous apparition. She is savage and superb, he tells us, wild-eyed and magnificent. She treads the earth proudly, her body covered with barbarous ornaments, her hair arranged in the shape of a helmet. For Marlow she embodies the spirit of the dark forests: 'And in the hush that had fallen suddenly upon the whole sorrowful land, the immense wilderness, the colossal body of the fecund and mysterious life seemed to look at her, pensive, as though it had been looking at the image of its own tenebrous and passionate soul.' She regards pilgrims on Marlow's steamer without a stir, 'like the wilderness itself, with an air of brooding over an inscrutable purpose'.

If we compare this splendid savage with Kurtz's European fiancée, his Intended, it may seem that we are setting side by side dynamic energy with sterile hypocrisy, life with death. The savage is tragic and fierce; we may take it for granted that Kurtz has enjoyed sexual orgies with her in his role as a worshipped god to whom human sacrifices are offered. Her Dionysiac passions might seem more attractive in their vitality than the living tomb the Intended has created for herself in Brussels. As often in Conrad, objects associated with human beings take on appropriate characteristics. The Intended lives in a house in a street as still and decorous as a well-kept alley in a cemetery. Her tall marble fireplace has a cold and monumental whiteness, and her grand piano gleams like a sombre and polished sarcophagus. She has chosen for herself a graveyard, where she can exist in comfort only through a lie; her condition symbolizes that of Western Europe. In contrast, the savage lives out her sexual urges as naturally as if she were a wild beast.

Yet there is something detestable, even loathsome, about this primitive creature. The youthful Russian, whom Kurtz befriends in the forest, tells Marlow how she wanted him killed for taking rags from the storeroom to mend his clothes. The unspeakable rites in which she has participated presumably include torture and killings. Co-habitation with this superb but mindless creature degrades Kurtz; for Conrad's total response to her, as to the wilderness, mixes together the attractive and the repellent.

The novel can be interpreted in a Freudian manner as a journey into the wilderness of sex, a fantasy shaped by Conrad's own divided impulses. The pilgrims penetrate down a narrow channel to find, in the darkness, a violent orgiastic experience. Kurtz, the outlaw-figure, has dared to transgress the restraints imposed by civilization. He represents Marlow's shadow self, the secret sharer, and the voyage of exploration is a night journey into the unconscious, or a discovery of the Freudian Id. From this point of view, the imprecision of Conrad's language in descriptions of the wilderness could be a sub-conscious evasion of the truth, a fascinated hovering around a subject whose realities he dare not fully acknowledge. Elsewhere, as Bernard Meyer has shown, Conrad's reaction to sex seems masochistic and fearful. The helmet-like hair is characteristic of other Conrad heroines, notably Felicia Moorsom in 'The Planter of Malata', whose lover enjoys self-abasement before her power. Should we interpret the whole fearful journey, therefore, as a sign of Conrad's repressed nightmares, his desire for a sexual initiation whose demands might prove him impotent?

When such Freudian interpretations are put forward as complete explanations, they become reductive. Conrad's impressionist method gathers into itself a wealth of possible meanings of which the Freudian constitute only a part. Nor do I agree with E. M. Forster or F. R. Leavis, who find the treatment of the wilderness too imprecise. The darkness exists as a literary symbol, whose paraphrasable meanings can never do full justice to the richness of this poetic meditation on human existence. The novel contrasts the savage woman with the Intended, Western civilization with Africa, the language of the rational mind, of concrete imagery and recognizable forms, with a mystery at the heart of consciousness beyond expression in words. Like Marlow, we are offered a choice of nightmares, but the strategy of the novel suggests that final commitment is possible only for the simple and the deluded. The story is a powerful fable of the divided consciousness, of the warring values of passion and restraint.

—C. B. Cox, *Joseph Conrad: The Modern Imagination* (London: J. M. Dent & Sons, 1974), pp. 45–47

✤

Cedric Watts on the Ambiguity of the Title of *Heart of Darkness*

[Cedric Watts, a lecturer in the School of English and American Studies at the University of Sussex, is the author of *The English Novel* (1976), *Joseph Conrad: A Literary Life* (1989), and several monographs on Shakespeare's plays. In this extract, Watts reflects on the ambiguity of the title of *Heart of Darkness*.]

When the tale was first published, as a serial in *Blackwood's Magazine* in 1899, the title was *The Heart of Darkness*. Obviously enough, the title-phrase can mean "the centre of a dark (sinister, evil, corrupt, malevolent, mysterious or obscure) region". But because of the ambiguity of the word "of", the phrase can also mean "the heart which has the quality of darkness", suggesting a human being with a dark (sinister, evil, corrupt, malevolent, mysterious or obscure) inner nature. The presence of "*The*" in the original title appears to tilt the balance, so that most readers would probably have sensed at once the former meaning and overlooked (until they were well embarked on the narrative) the latter. However, for the ensuing publication in book form, Conrad deleted "*The*"; and by thus making the grammatical format of the phrase resemble that of such phrases as "man of straw" or "hearts of oak", he gave an equipoise of ambiguity to the title. The very equipoise is functionally valuable, holding us briefly in doubt as we begin the tale, and appropriately heralding some of the duplicities of effect to come. ⟨. . .⟩

Several of Conrad's works have titles which invite such discrimination. The title of *Nostromo,* for example, which means "our man" and is the name given to the apparently devoted employee of the company, accumulates ironic force, since Nostromo's final loyalty is to himself only—and in such self-devotion he can be regarded as betraying himself. Yet when he had been loyal to the company, had he not been betraying himself then, by letting himself be the patronized puppet of capitalism? In these ways the title serves as the nexus of several questions about loyalty to others and to one's own best possibilities, about solidarity, identity, and ownership. In the case of *The Secret Agent,* the title initially seems to have innocuously specific reference, but its connotations gradually undergo ironic expansion. It brings to mind Verloc himself—yet his activities as an agent are not secret from the police; then Winnie Verloc, whose secret and intense devotion to her brother is eventually the cause of her husband's death; and finally the hidden force of abstract "agents" like human madness and despair.

But unlike these later examples, the title *Heart of Darkness* offers not simply alternative readings in retrospect, but also, from the start, a certain disturbing mysteriousness through the immediate possibility of alternative glosses: we sense ambiguity even before consciously analysing the components of the phrase. And, throughout the tale, ambiguities proliferate in the areas of semantics (as when Marlow plays upon the different meanings of "absurd"), of association or connotation of imagery (as will now be discussed), and of character, motive and action. The title thus strikes the keynote, resonant, mysterious and equivocal, for one of the most intensely orchestrated works of fiction. "Dark", "darkness": the words re-echo to the very last paragraph, in which "the tranquil waterway leading to the uttermost ends of the earth flowed sombre under an overcast sky—seemed to lead into the heart of an immense darkness".

In *Heart of Darkness,* corruption and evil are subversive and tentacular: they send out tentacles which entwine themselves about and amongst the seemingly sound and good. This effect stems largely from a principle which Cleanth Brooks defined when he was discussing *The Waste Land.* Brooks said that T. S. Eliot there "works in terms of surface parallelisms which in reality make ironical contrasts, and in terms of surface contrasts which in reality constitute parallelisms". These words describe exactly the principle that Conrad uses in deploying the substantially but not entirely different materials of *Heart of Darkness.* Later I will be discussing many examples of this principle; for the present I wish to point out that it is partly applicable to the way in which Conrad exploits the primary and secondary literary connotations of "light", "darkness", "black" and "white".

"And God said, Let there be light . . . . ." "Light" has the most ancient of associations with Godhead, sanctity and truth ("enlightenment"); and "darkness" has long connoted evil, death, the sinister, ignorance, error, and the oppressively mysterious. "White" has associations with holiness, purity, chastity; and "black" with evil, damnation, sin. Thus is formed a reassuringly simplistic balance of primary connotations which Conrad repeatedly evokes and upsets: upsets by intermittently exploiting secondary connotations. St. Matthew (chapter 23, verse 27) had likened hypocrites to whited sepulchres, which indeed appear beautiful outward, but are within full of dead *men's* bones, and of all uncleanness"; and in the tale, white is the colour of Fresleven's bleached bones, of the skulls round Kurtz's hut, of Kurtz's bald head, of the ivory which elicits the pilgrims' avarice; and the city which contains the company's headquarters reminds Marlow of "a whited sepulchre". The signal examples of corruption are not among the blacks but among the white men, who are responsible for colouring-in the "white patch" that once, Marlow reminds us, filled the map of the dark continent.

—Cedric Watts, *Conrad's* Heart of Darkness: *A Critical and Contextual Discussion* (Milan, Italy: Mursia International, 1977), pp. 7, 9–10

✤

Chinua Achebe on Conrad's Use of Africa in *Heart of Darkness*

[Chinua Achebe (b. 1930), a distinguished Nigerian novelist, is a professor emeritus at the University of

Nigeria. Among his best-known novels are *Things Fall Apart* (1958) and *A Man of the People* (1966). In this extract, Achebe argues that Conrad uses Africa as a contrast to the enlightenment of Western civilization.]

Heart of Darkness projects the image of Africa as "the other world," the antithesis of Europe and therefore of civilization, a place where a man's vaunted intelligence and refinement are finally mocked by triumphant bestiality. The book opens on the River Thames, tranquil, resting peacefully "at the decline of day after ages of good service done to the race that peopled its banks." But the actual story takes place on the River Congo, the very antithesis of the Thames. The River Congo is quite decidedly not a River Emeritus. It has rendered no service and enjoys no old-age pension. We are told that "going up that river was like travelling back to the earliest beginning of the world."

Is Conrad saying then that these two rivers are very different, one good, the other bad? Yes, but that is not the real point. What actually worries Conrad is the lurking hint of kinship, of common ancestry. For the Thames, too, "has been one of the dark places of the earth." It conquered its darkness, of course, and is now at peace. But if it were to visit its primordial relative, the Congo, it would run the terrible risk of hearing grotesque, suggestive echoes of its own forgotten darkness, and of falling victim to an avenging recrudescence of the mindless frenzy of the first beginnings.

I am not going to waste your time with examples of Conrad's famed evocation of the African atmosphere. In the final consideration it amounts to no more than a steady, ponderous, fake-ritualistic repetition of two sentences, one about silence and the other about frenzy. An example of the former is "It was the stillness of an implacable force brooding over an inscrutable intention" and of the latter, "The steamer toiled along slowly on the edge of a black and incomprehensible frenzy." Of course, there is a judicious change of adjective from time to time so that instead of "inscrutable," for example, you might have "unspeakable," etc., etc.

The eagle-eyed English critic, F. R. Leavis, drew attention nearly thirty years ago to Conrad's "adjectival insistence upon inexpressible and incomprehensible mystery." That insistence must not be dismissed lightly, as many Conrad critics have tended to do, as a mere stylistic flaw. For it raises serious questions of artistic good faith. When a writer, while pretending to record scenes, incidents and their impact, is in reality engaged in inducing hypnotic stupor in his readers through a bombardment of emotive words and other forms of trickery much more has to be at stake than stylistic felicity. Generally, normal readers are well armed to detect and resist such underhand activity. But Conrad chose his subject well—one which was guaranteed not to put him in conflict with the psychological predisposition of his readers or raise the need for him to contend with their resistance. He chose the role of purveyor of comforting myths.

The most interesting and revealing passages in *Heart of Darkness* are, however, about people. I must quote a long passage from the middle of the story in which representatives of Europe in a steamer going down the Congo encounter the denizens of Africa:

> We were wanderers on a prehistoric earth, on an earth that wore the aspect of an unknown planet. We could have fancied ourselves the first of men taking possession of an accursed inheritance, to be subdued at the cost of profound anguish and of excessive toil. But suddenly, as we struggled round a bend, there would be a glimpse of rush walls, of peaked grass-roofs, a burst of yells, a whirl of black limbs, a mass of hands clapping, of feet stamping, of bodies swaying, of eyes rolling, under the droop of heavy and motionless foliage. The steamer toiled along slowly on the edge of a black and incomprehensible frenzy. The prehistoric man was cursing us, praying to us, welcoming us—who could tell? We were cut off from the comprehension of our surroundings; we glided past like phantoms, wondering and secretly appalled, as sane men would be before an enthusiastic outbreak in a madhouse. We could not remember because we were travelling in the night of first ages, of those ages that are gone, leaving hardly a sign—and no memories.
>
> The earth seemed unearthly. We are accustomed to look upon the shackled form of a conquered monster, but there—there you could look at a thing monstrous and free. It was unearthly, and the men were—No, they were not inhuman. Well, you know, that was the worst of it—this suspicion of their not being inhuman. It would come slowly to one. They howled and leaped, and spun, and made horrid faces; but what thrilled

> you was just the thought of your remote kinship with this wild and passionate uproar. Ugly. Yes, it was ugly enough; but if you were man enough you would admit to yourself that there was in you just the faintest trace of a response to the terrible frankness of that noise, a dim suspicion of there being a meaning in it which you—you so remote from the night of first ages—could comprehend.

Herein lies the meaning of *Heart of Darkness* and the fascination it holds over the Western mind: "What thrilled you was just the thought of their humanity—like yours. . . . Ugly."

—Chinua Achebe, "An Image of Africa," *Massachusetts Review* 18, No. 4 (Winter 1977): 783–85

✤

WALTER J. ONG ON THE ENDING OF *HEART OF DARKNESS*

[Walter J. Ong (b. 1912) is a former professor of English at St. Louis University. He has written *The Barbarian Within and Other Fugitive Essays* (1962) and *Faith and Contexts* (1992). In this extract, Ong reflects on Kurtz's last words and the ending of *Heart of Darkness*.]

The resolution of the story in *Heart of Darkness* is in many ways enigmatic, yet it has commonly been understood that the climactic statement about Kurtz's last words, made in Marlow's report to Kurtz's fiancée, Kurtz's "Intended," is essential to what the tale is "about" and that this statement was an out-and-out lie. But was it? The question will lead into the issues just mentioned—colonialism, racism, antifeminism—into them and out again.

At first blush, Marlow's final report to Kurtz's "Intended" indeed appears to be a lie, and conspicuously a lie. From Conrad's text the reader learns how Marlow tells the Intended, anxious, expectant, poised in well-gowned mourning in the lofty European drawing-room, that Kurtz's last word was her name, whereas the reader knows from Marlow's earlier account that Kurtz's last words in fact had been "The horror! The horror!" But lies come cheap and they are not essentially moving. The climactic effect of this closing incident in Marlow's tale cannot be explained in terms of a simple lapse into dishonesty on Marlow's part. If this is a lie, it is not any old lie. The effect of Marlow's reply, felt by the reader for the most part subconsciously, comes largely from the shocking equivalence which the reply establishes: Marlow has interchanged the cry "The horror! The horror!" and the name of Kurtz's fiancée—and done so without ever pronouncing her name, which he refers to only as "your name" and which consequently Marlow's hearers and Conrad's readers never do learn. The name of the Intended remains a permanent blank in the story, a blank which can only be filled in by "The horror! The horror!"

This substitution is of course exquisite irony. But at what level? In this story irony is the rule, and any interpretation risks oversimplicity. Even more than most narratives of Conrad's this one is delivered layer within layer, Conrad's own sensibility encasing Conrad's persona or narrator's voice, whose story encases Marlow's, which in turn encases Kurtz's story, itself first delivered in snatches to Marlow by a medley of exiled voices and finally distorted by the voice of the girl, projecting Kurtz in her own way.

Heart of Darkness consists of a web of voices, of cries and responses, often explicitly called to the reader's attention to establish multi-layered involvement and mystery. Kurtz first enters the story through the voices of others: Marlow muses, "He was just a voice for me." When Kurtz appears, his voice takes over in a world of many voices: "He was very little more than a voice. And I heard—him—it—this voice—other voices—all of them were so little more than voices." "You don't talk with that man [Kurtz]—you listen to him." "We talked of everything." "A deep voice [of the ailing Kurtz, at Marlow's first encounter with him] reached me faintly." And so on and on. Has anyone counted the times voice is mentioned in the story? "A voice! A voice! It rang deep to the very last." Kurtz's last recorded act is his final utterance. Kurtz is dead, Marlow goes on eating his dinner. "The voice was gone. What else had been there?" More than a year after Kurtz's death, asked by the girl what Kurtz's last words were, Marlow thinks of her present sorrow as coinciding in time with Kurtz's dying voice: "I saw them together—I heard them together." Then Marlow speaks the crucial words.

At the same time, voice is not all. At points, visual impressions compete with auditory and other, or dominate the narrative. The story is set in light and dark polarities, as critics have uniformly noted. Through the closing scene especially, Marlow's encounter with Kurtz's fiancée, the reader is explicitly and repeatedly made to attend to darkness, light, dusk, luminosity, murkiness, and a host of other light-dark qualities. The title of the story flits all through the text, but especially toward the end: "the beating of a heart—the heart of a conquering darkness," "panic in my heart . . . the room was growing darker . . . darkness deepened." With its closing words, "into the heart of an immense darkness," the narrative enters forever into the mystery announced by its title.

On the surface Kurtz's adventure had appeared simple enough: serving commercial interests, he goes, an extraordinarily talented and engaging European, to the then Belgian Congo, where, indulging what today might be described as an "ego trip," he deteriorates morally, "goes native," is brought back seriously ill from his station in the interior, and dies, expressing with his last words the horror of the state of soul in which he ultimately finds himself. Marlow's part appears also simple enough on the surface: coming to the Congo, he hears of and meets Kurtz, empathizes with Kurtz's deathbed expression of horror, and lies to Kurtz's fiancee to keep her from becoming aware, uselessly, of Kurtz's moral collapse. But the echoing of voices and the constant chiaroscuro in the imagery of the narrative hint that all is not so straightforward: being a European and "going native" are both puzzling routines and at points blur with each other. It is the Thames, where Marlow and his listeners had shipped and were awaiting the turn of the tide, not the Congo, that flows at the end of the story "into the heart of an immense darkness." The Thames slips into the sea, where its waters and those of the Congo are one. The last message to the reader is that the whole business of the narrative is enigmatic. Ford Madox Ford has rehearsed how he anguished with Conrad over the exact wording of the final paragraph of this tale, a paragraph which Ford believed was the finest thing in all of Conrad's early work.

Conrad's own suggested hermeneutic for dealing with the enigma of his tale is itself paradoxical, for, though a secret or a mystery or an enigma is normally inwardness, Conrad's persona—the narrator who tells about Marlow and retells Marlow's story—says that Marlow's enigmas have their explanations not within themselves but without. To Marlow, as we read at the beginning of the story, "the meaning of an episode was not inside like a kernel, but outside, enveloping the tale which brought it out only as a glow brings out a haze." Kurtz's Intended is in a curious way the haze outside, which the narrative illuminates. Far beyond Africa, in the lofty European drawing room, Marlow meets her when "the dusk was falling." Within Conrad's hermeneutic, her physical setting is an obvious analogue for her role in the narrative: she catches the glow of the tale. The figure of the Intended concentrates the meaning of Africa and of Kurtz—and, more significantly, of Marlow. For this story, as Albert Guérard has correctly pointed out, is not about Africa or Kurtz or Kurtz's fiancée, but about Marlow himself.

Illuminated, the Intended is still hazy. Still, she reveals meanings—hazily. This she does chiefly because of the context of the question she puts to Marlow and because of the answer she elicits from him. And the paradox of paradoxes here—absolutely crucial in the story's depths, though unnoticed I believe by commentators thus far, perhaps because Western eyes turned to Africa have been so pitifully clouded, even Conrad's consciously controlled eyes, though his heart, his unconscious, was dead right—is that, however it may appear at the surface or just beneath the outermost wrappings, Marlow's response to her, his last recorded words to her, his assurance to her that Kurtz's final utterance was her name, at its deepest level was not a lie at all. It was in itself the starkest truth, but, in the story, veiled. By what? Almost everything, in the story and outside.

—Walter J. Ong, "Truth in Conrad's Darkness," *Mosaic* 11, No. 1 (Fall 1977): 152–55

✤

Garrett Stewart on Nightmares in *Heart of Darkness*

[Garrett Stewart (b. 1945) is a professor of English at the University of California at Santa Barbara. He is the author of *Dickens and the Trials of the Imagination* (1974) and *Death Sentences: Styles of Dying in British Fiction* (1984). In this extract, Stewart explores Marlow's self-deceptions in his journey to Kurtz and Conrad's use of a nightmare motif in *Heart of Darkness*.]

Marlow repeatedly describes his experience in Africa, and especially with Kurtz, as a "nightmare," and this is never more telling a metaphor than in Marlow's drawing back from the ultimate fate of Kurtz. Psychological truism has it that we never dream our own death, even in the worst of nightmares—that we always wake to consciousness within an inch or so of the abyss. So with Marlow's nightmare. We can neither dream nor, according to Freud, even force ourselves to imagine with any cogency our own demise. Marlow, therefore, must wake up from another's fatal nightmare just in the nick of time's tilting over into eternity. Only later is the lie of idealism unconsciously resurrected from its own death scene in order to be traded on as the barter of return, the inevitably exacted price of repatriation to the European community. Kurtz's revelation is a sweeping death sentence, the end point of an asymptotic nightmare that Marlow holds off in order to come back and go on. Kurtz's abject but profound darkness dims to a "grey skepticism" in Marlow that is not only the trivialization but the very ticket of return.

If, back at the sepulchral hub of Europe, the Intended's dark counterspecter, that feminine apparition from our savage source, might only be held to a shadowy depth that does not impinge so remorselessly on consciousness, the woman of Faith might still manage to embody for Marlow an ideal he could "bow down before," offer his own misguided and mortal "sacrifice" to in the form of that deadly lie. As he said earlier of Kurtz: "I laid the ghost of his gifts at last with a lie." These gifts of insight into darkness must be laid to rest, or else Marlow would have nothing left to revere. Kurtz's revelation of "the horror" is fatally incompatible with genuflection. Since we know that Marlow's own idol-like person seems an outward sign of such internalized idealism, internalized at the expense of full truth, we sense the reflexivity: "bowing my head before the faith that was in her, before that great and saving illusion that shone with an unearthly glow in the darkness, in the triumphant darkness from which I could not defend her—from which I could not even defend myself." With devious valor, however, he attempts this self-defense, and by preserving such a feminine dreamworld he hopes to prevent his own from "getting worse," making good the grammatical and psychic parallelism in "defend her . . . defend myself." For Marlow (to risk again the boxing off of a more expressive complexity) is ultimately homo quadruplex, a wholeness reified into the mental powers of assimilation (as well as repression) played off against lower and would-be higher functions: mind against body in the helmsman, heart or soul in Kurtz, and finally a supervening and repressive Faith in the Intended. In this fourfold "allegory," eventually unfolded, she represents pure idealist intentionality preserved against the corrosive truth of experience, but preserved by being interred along with the buried truth in a sarcophagal unreality.

Daleski follows his critique of Conrad's coda with this sentence: "Consequently, it is difficult for us to make any meaningful connection between the lie and death." But we are now in a position to make this connection amid the metaphors of spiritual deadliness and posthumous defeatism that litter the coda as much as they do the tale itself. Marlow's untruth is lethal precisely because it kills the meaning of a death. There is a corollary to the proposition that lying is a kind of dying. Truth, even grasped only in death, is a defiance of death, a notion hallowed in British fiction's treatment of demise. Kurtz's self-realization, about the "horror" his life and death would have epitomized, rendered his image deathless in the mind, a perennial admonishing phantom, except that the lie kills it. Partly to abet Marlow in this homicidal denial, two of the most trusted mortuary formulas of fiction, each a version of death by epitome, are invoked with some verbal and thematic deviousness in connection with Kurtz's death, one early, one late. When Marlow realizes that the name Kurtz, meaning "short" in German, is belied by the man's considerable height, he says—

as if forgetting (because wanting to, no doubt) the cauterizing truth telling of Kurtz's last utterance—that "the name was as true as everything else in his life—and death." Marlow's own retrospective account seems colored, obscured, by the late meliorating lie eventually summoned to slay Kurtz's black epiphany. Marlow does, however, recognize the "true" consonance of Kurtz's life and death in another sense, for the persistent specter of Kurtz's ghost calls up this postmortem observation: "He lived then before me; he lived as much as he had ever lived . . . a shadow darker than the shadow of the night." Ghostliness is at one with his ghastly aura in life. There is further evidence in the coda that Conrad, if not Marlow, has the mortuary tradition in literature specifically in mind, with its often rigorous equations between death and identity. When, hoping for solace, the Intended clutches at the time-tested heroic prescription, "He died as he lived," Marlow's mock iteration, "His end was in every way worthy of his life," not only secretly reverses the moral judgment implicit in her faith, even as he preserves some of that faith for her and for himself, but helps us see the additional irony to which Marlow, in the throes of untruth, is no doubt blinded. The epitomizing apothegm of death is traditionally phrased with a change in tense—"He died as he *had* lived"—with pluperfect brought to perfection (in the existential sense) in the preterit. The Intended, however, has unwittingly summarized the nature of a corrupt life coextensive with death and equivalent to it: the long-pending end of a man who, again, "died as he lived." Living a lie of moral superiority, lies being deadly, Kurtz died *while* he lived ("as" in this sense), his death scene true to life in its very deadliness. What Céline would call "death on the installment plan" is, however, a truth about Kurtz that is itself sabotaged and assassinated.

—Garrett Stewart, "Lying as Dying in *Heart of Darkness*," *PMLA* 95, No. 3 (May 1980): 328–30

WILLIAM M. HAGEN ON *HEART OF DARKNESS* AND *APOCALYPSE NOW*

[William M. Hagen is a professor of English at Oklahoma Baptist University. In this extract, Hagen analyzes the use of Conrad's *Heart of Darkness* in Francis Ford Coppola's film *Apocalypse Now.*]

Toward the end of *Apocalypse Now* we reach that supremely Conradian moment when Willard, the Marlow figure, confronts the object of his journey, Colonel Kurtz. Does he come to rescue Kurtz and, in so doing, test himself? If Francis Ford Coppola had chosen to follow Joseph Conrad here, he might have gotten some desperately needed U.S. military assistance. But that was not the kind of script conclusion the director of *The Godfather* and *Godfather II* had planned for his war epic.

Still, Coppola underscores the significance of the meeting by altering his style. When Willard is taken into the temple for the first time, the whole pace of the film slows down, as if in imitation of the ponderous immensity of Brando. Brando-Kurtz slowly emerges into the light and pats water on his gleaming bald head, in a kind of ritual cleansing. The camera holds the shots for a much longer period than usual, allowing movement to be dictated by the actors rather than by focusing in or editing. Dialogue too proceeds at a much slower pace, with pauses occurring within sentences as well as between them. Questions are left hanging for a few extra beats, even when there is nothing particularly threatening about them. Of course, the pace has been slackening ever since the Do Lung Bridge sequence, but this scene is so slow it borders on worship. Brando is meant to be mythic, the still center of darkness, worshipped and self-worshipping, capable of every atrocity including self-annihilation through his double. Willard is so affected by the atmosphere of disorder and stasis, that he has to force himself to kill Kurtz. Through lighting, camera angles, and crosscutting, the murder itself is transformed into a kind of dance in and out of darkness, creating a visual-aesthetic experience quite as isolated as the slow-motion destruction of a Sam Peckinpah film. The acquiescence of Kurtz and the preliminary appearance of Willard out of black water make the whole affair a kind of rite of rebirth-initiation into the world of Kurtz through slaying of the king.

With the exception of the rather abrupt thematic cross-cuts between the murder and the ritual killing of a caribou, the encounters are quite stunning and organic . . . visually. We could perhaps accept the deliberate departure from Conrad's novel if the director did not also seek to build in the psychological-moral dimensions of *Heart of Darkness.* His characters may be caught in a ritual of death and rebirth, but he wants them to have depth all the same. He wants viewers to confront the immensity of this war one more time. Above all, he wants to explain everything through Kurtz. So Coppola picks up Kurtz' last words and tries to build a structural theme for the last portion of the film. By the time we hear "The horror!" for the last time, in a memory replay, we are likely to have worked up that fine wrath normally reserved for all those who quote outrageously out of context.

Conrad's Kurtz mouths his last words as a message to himself and, through Marlow, to the world. He has not really explained himself to Marlow before this final exclamation. Through Marlow's summary and moral reactions, we come to a sense of the possibilities of meaning rather than definite meaning. The message is more Marlow's and the reader's than it is Kurtz'. By contrast, Kurtz precisely defines "horror"; the only way we can make his definition our message is to see his horror and enact his definition with Willard. The way to judgment lies through vicarious violence. Judgment is self-judgment.

The problem with even this transaction is that Willard seems almost unmoved by his experience. He certainly expresses no moral judgment. The worst he says is that he sees "no method" in Kurtz' operations. This statement may strike the reader of Conrad as uncomfortably similar to the Station Manager's amoral judgment of Kurtz' atrocities as merely "unsound" or bad for company business. The separation of reason from civilized morality, the fragmentation of the self so typical of the technocrat, causes Marlow to prefer the nightmare of Kurtz. Better to commit atrocities passionately than to account them wrong on grounds of efficiency. Like Dante—whose traditional moral hierarchy he reflects—Marlow can summon up a measure of sympathy for those who succumb to their emotions or appetites and reserve unmeasured scorn for those who pervert reason. Within the film, only the general at the briefing and Chef show the rational or emotional repugnance toward Kurtz; Willard, the professional soldier, is more than halfway friendly with this horror. After Chef joins the heads and Willard becomes part of the horror, we may realize that the whole point of the scenes at the Kurtz compound is to make the audience confront Kurtz' horror without moral mediation. From the very beginning, the shots of the compound were carefully filled with more separate images and actions, especially around the edges of the frame, than the eye could integrate. The eye was always kept moving and focusing on different parts of the screen. We did not have Marlow's field glasses or his sensibility to distance us or focus in sympathetically; we were entrapped and overwhelmed in an amoral medium range. Thus, instead of judgment or self-judgment, we are likely to come away from this perceptual overdose with the feeling that it has been a bad trip, and nothing more.

—William M. Hagen, "*Heart of Darkness* and the Process of *Apocalypse Now*," *Conradiana* 13, No. 1 (1981): 45–46

FRED MADDEN ON HORROR AND CORRUPTION IN *HEART OF DARKNESS*

[Fred Madden is a professor of English at Ithaca College and the author of articles on Edgar Allan Poe and Ken Kesey. In this extract, Madden studies the ending of *Heart of Darkness*, claiming that it underscores Marlow's sense of horror at the corruption that lies at the foundation of human life.]

Previous to the final interview, Marlow accepted Kurtz's dying whisper as a judgment against the corruption inherent in existence. But Marlow is not ready to deny the humanity of others as Kurtz did (emblematically indicated by the heads of the natives on stakes surrounding Kurtz's hut). Before the final interview, Marlow had interpreted Kurtz's dying repetition as representing two separate horrors: the horror of the universal triumph of corruption and the horror of "the adventures of [Kurtz's] own soul," a soul which acted as an agent in furthering corruption. In the final interview, however, Marlow realizes Kurtz's justice is without mercy because it is a justice which furthers corruption. Had Marlow followed "the nightmare of his choice" throughout the interview, the heavens would have "fallen" because Marlow would have lost his only option of resisting corruption and exercising restraint.

In refraining from telling Kurtz's Intended the truth, Marlow exercises restraint in refusing to corrupt others. Marlow's lie, however, is not an attempt to protect Kurtz's Intended from eventual corruption. Conrad gives the reader enough suggestions in the imagery of the interview to promote the feeling that she will not escape. As the interview proceeds, the images of "darkness" connected with her increase until she becomes "the whisper of a voice speaking from beyond the threshold of eternal darkness." Here Conrad is making an obvious parallel between the Intended and Kurtz who has been earlier described as a "voice" who hid "the barren darkness of his heart."

Both Kurtz and his Intended are described as voices speaking in darkness, as is Marlow himself aboard the *Nellie.* But during the course of his narrative, Marlow is able to pin-point man's sole hope of resisting inevitable corruption: it lies neither in Kurtz's "justice" nor in his Intended's naiveté. For Marlow (and Conrad), man must refrain from becoming an agent of corruption. At the end of his journey Marlow comes to accept the almost paradoxical realization that man must refrain from furthering the spread of corruption while acquiescing to its inevitability. In an action similar to Mrs. Gould's refusal to reveal the truth about Nostromo's corruption to Dr. Monygham, Marlow refrains from telling Kurtz's Intended the truth. In both novels, Conrad is advocating man's acceptance of a limited, imperfect, and corruptible existence. In Marlow's case, the compassion which leads to this acceptance must be judged morally preferable to Kurtz's form of "justice" or the Company's inhuman machinery of exploitation. Marlow's growth and final realization, in which "observer" becomes "participant," knowledge becomes wisdom, suggest the necessity of "restraint" and compassion as counterforces to man's propensity to exploit others. But "restraint" must derive from the individual in the face of the double horrors in *Heart of Darkness,* the inevitable outward and inward corruption of all that mankind values. This "restraint" also must continue in the certain knowledge that it is, at best, merely a gesture against overwhelming forces, and for the reader of *Heart of Darkness* this gesture is all that illuminates Conrad's vision.

—Fred Madden, "Marlow and the Double Horror in *Heart of Darkness,*" *Midwest Quarterly* 27, No. 4 (Summer 1986): 516–17

✤

BARBARA JOHNSON AND MARJORIE GARBER ON PSYCHOANALYSIS AND "THE SECRET SHARER"

[Barbara Johnson (b. 1947), a professor of French and comparative literature at Harvard University, is a distinguished contemporary literary critic and theorist. Among her many books are *The Critical Difference* (1980) and *A World of Difference* (1987). Marjorie Garber (b. 1944) is a professor of English at Harvard University and the author of *Coming of Age in Shakespeare* (1981) and *Vested Interests: Cross-Dressing and Cultural Anxiety* (1992). In this extract, Johnson and Garber examine the psychological elements of "The Secret Sharer," specifically the two versions of the murder story told by Leggatt and Archbold.]

When we turn to the second paradigm of psychoanalytic reading, the pathology of the character, we discover a very similar Oedipal conflict in Conrad's "The Secret Sharer." If by Oedipal we mean competition with or rivalry with a father or father figure, or, by extension, threatening figures who wield power and seem to disempower the protagonist, the story has more than enough such conflicts to offer. There are several candidates for the role of father, notably the chief mate on the ship, an older man with "a terrible growth of whisker," "round eyes and frightful whiskers," like many emblems of castration in Freud (e.g., "The Head of the Medusa," "The Uncanny"), and, later, the skipper of the *Sephora,* also older, also whiskered, a married man whose name might be Archbold (a splendidly potent name) but the narrator isn't sure—he has repressed it, and explains away the repression: "at this distance of years I hardly am sure." . . . "Captain Archbold (if that was his name)."

At the inception of the story, before the arrival of either Leggatt (the double) or "Archbold" (if that is his name, the nameless, almost named, figure of fatherhood and the Law), it is the chief mate who seems to threaten the narrator's authority. He is obsessed by uncanny castration images—the mate's whiskers, the scorpion in the inkwell—and beset by doubts. Do I have the right to be alone with my ship? Is my command secure? Aren't the father figures around me going to do me harm? As the story opens, the young captain has decided on a demonstration of his own self-sufficient super-potency. He will stay awake himself, rather than set an anchor watch, and assume command of the sleeping ship. Feeling better, determined "in those solitary hours of the night to get on terms with the ship of which I knew nothing, manned by men of whom I knew very little more," he relaxes enough to take heart from "the reasonable thought that the ship was like other ships, the men like other men." Heartened, he thinks of smoking a cigar ("Arriving at that comforting conclusion, I bethought myself of a cigar and went below to get it". Sometimes a cigar, when fetched from "below," from the unconscious, is more than a cigar. He stands confidently on the deck, barefoot, in his sleeping suit, "a glowing cigar in my teeth," the picture of male potency (or of infancy imitating male potency). At this point he notices something dangling from the side of the ship, something that shouldn't be there—the rope ladder. He realizes with annoyance that it is his fault the thing is hanging out—since he dismissed the watch—and that he'd better put it back in before anyone notices, since it is a sign of inefficient command. The excessive object thus doubles the cigar: the display of the phallus is both desirable and punishable. "I asked myself whether it was wise ever to interfere with the established routine of duties even from the kindest of motives. My action might have made me appear eccentric. Goodness only knew how that absurdly whiskered mate would 'account' for my conduct, and what the whole ship thought of the informality of their new captain. I was vexed with myself." Consumed with anxiety, with castration fears, he sees something in the water, and the cigar drops out of his mouth.

> I saw at once something elongated and pale floating very close to the ladder. Before I could form a guess a faint flash of phosphorescent light, which seemed to issue suddenly from the naked body of a man, flickered in the sleeping water with the elusive, silent play of summer lightning in a night sky. With a gasp I saw revealed to my stare a pair of feet, long legs, a broad livid back immersed right up to the neck in a greenish cadaverous glow. One hand, awash, clutched the bottom rung of the ladder. He was complete but for the head. A headless corpse! The cigar dropped out of my gaping mouth with a tiny plop and a short hiss.

The cigar drops out of his gaping mouth at the image of the headless corpse, the apparent realization of his castration fears. He is going to be punished by the whiskered mate and others for what he has done—or failed to do. But then the body's head appears, and, as in the Medusa story, he is released from his condition of stony paralysis: "it was enough for the horrid, frost-bound sensation which had gripped me about the chest to pass off." He is still intact—and so is the other. He is not guilty; indeed, it is the *other* man who is guilty, and guilty of murder, the murder of a "father" figure, the murder the narrator in part desires but won't and can't permit. Arriving at this point in the young captain's train of thought and complex of fears, Leggatt represents the part of the narrator he can't accept or integrate. The dilemma is posed; shall I integrate him? Shall I acknowledge him as part of myself? If I do, then I can perhaps have a sense of proportion about the guilt I thought was so unacknowledgable. I will not be totally innocent, but I will be able to take command without feeling so threatened by catastrophe. I will understand that the law is often absurd—that to take command is to be able to assume guilt and to issue arbitrary orders, to let the symptom go (open the portholes, sail too close to land).

The two versions of the murder story the narrator hears, one from Leggatt, the other from "Archbold," are both his fantasies. In one, Leggatt's story, the ship is in danger, the captain impotent and ineffectual, unable to give the order to reef the foresail, the other man is obstructive; he, Leggatt, acts heroically in the face of the fathers' failure, eliminates the obstruction, and saves the ship. In the other story, told by the skipper of the *Sephora,* it is the young chief mate, the rebellious son, who must be punished and disowned:

> "You see, he wasn't exactly the sort for the chief mate of a ship like the *Sephora."* I had become so connected in thoughts and impressions with the secret sharer of my cabin that I felt as if I, personally, were being given to understand that I, too, was not the sort that would have done for the chief mate of a ship like the *Sephora.*

Archbold would like to call Leggatt a suicide, to assume that he killed himself out of guilt. The "truth" of this primal scene is unrecoverable, and does not in fact exist; it exists only in its retellings, or rather in the narrator's retellings of those retellings, and both dramatize his unconscious fears, satisfy his unconscious needs: to be a hero; to be punished; to be a man; to be a child.

In the end, having harbored and released the fugitive, the young captain can be alone with the ship, with the command. He has come out the other end of the Oedipal crisis by accepting the necessity of losing a part of himself: his fantasy of guilty omnipotence. In essence he has arrived at a new, revisionary version of castration as *enabling.*

—Barbara Johnson and Marjorie Garber, "Secret Sharing: Reading Conrad Psychoanalytically," *College English* 49, No. 6 (October 1987): 632–34

Richard Ambrosini on Narrative Technique in *Heart of Darkness*

[Richard Ambrosini (b. 1955) is an English language assistant in the department of English at the University of Rome. He has translated Conrad's *An Outcast of the Islands* into Italian. In this extract from *Conrad's Fiction as Critical Discourse* (1991), Ambrosini studies the unreliability of Marlow as narrator and other narrative techniques in *Heart of Darkness.*]

The exchange between Marlow and the would-be-listener/frame narrator in the tale's opening provides the key for a reading of the different linguistic levels sketched by the narrative frame. The frame narrator has a double function in the first pages. His most explicit function includes the describing of the setting (the way he stresses the "bond of the sea"), introducing the characters, and reminding the reader that he is the same narrative voice of "Youth": "Between us there was, as I have already said somewhere, the bond of the sea." His second, more important function, begins when he launches into a rhapsodic hymn to the "spirit of the past" which the Thames evokes in a seaman. In this long passage he expresses views which were certainly also Conrad's, such as the actuality of the memories which form the tradition of the British navy "for a man who has, as the phrase goes, 'followed the sea' with reverence and affection." Conrad did indeed write, in "Legends" (1924), the essay he was working on when he died, that legends "are a form of memory . . . a fine form of imaginative recognition of the past." In "Tradition" (1918), he points out that it is "perhaps because I have not been born to the inheritance of [the Merchant Service] tradition . . . that I am so consciously aware of it." Understandably, then, some commentators have identified the frame narrator with Conrad himself. This identification, however, hinders a proper reading of Conrad's handling of the voice, of that irony which allows him to mingle those platitudes Marlow will later attack with insights inserted in the narration. When the frame narrator embroiders on the instinctive feelings arising from the sunset on the river, the legends become banners of civilization. At this point the frame narrator voices a kind of language which Marlow will later attack, a language which is part of the narrative frame, while the frame narrator's first reflections, we learn by contrast, were silent.

When Marlow first speaks it is immediately clear that he is pursuing a completely different thought. He has been thinking that "this also . . . has been one of the dark places of the earth."

And when he recalls the light which "came out of this river since," he stops to address the frame narrator, "you say Knights?", thus questioning the narrator's reference to "all the men of whom the nation is proud, from Sir Francis Drake to Sir John Franklin, knights all, titled and untitled—the great knights-errant of the sea." Conrad is clearly having Marlow question the frame narrator's generalization about how they all "looked at the venerable stream," differentiating the internal narrator's outlook from the one of his audience, and setting up that ironic perspective which characterizes the conflict between the wandering seaman and his listeners.

As the frame narrator's reliability is being undermined, his role changes again. Conrad uses his comments on what Marlow is saying to point out the way in which Marlow tells a story. Conrad maps out this strategy in the first pages through a series of duets and "asides" in which the critical discourse makes clear from the very beginning that in this tale the telling of the story is extremely problematical. The passages in which the tale's critical discourse is first made explicit are the frame narrator's famous disquisition about "the meaning of an episode" for Marlow, and the latter's own reminder that his first concern is with "the effect of [an experience] on me." The two passages cast light on one another, illuminating the implications of the narrative's dual quality.

Marlow is described, at first, in opposition to other seamen. He is a wanderer, they are "sedentary": their minds "are of the stay-at-home order" and their yarns "have a direct simplicity, the whole meaning of which lies within the shell of a cracked nut." Marlow spins yarns like any other seaman, but his stories—like his mind—are "not typical." For him, the frame narrator explains, "the meaning of an episode was not inside like a kernel but outside, enveloping the tale which brought it out only as a glow brings out a haze, in the likeness of one of these misty halos that sometimes are made visible by the spectral illumination of moonshine." The only way of obtaining a "meaning" would be to crack the tale's nutshell and thus extract the meaning one wants to find. The frame narrator is cautioning the readers about such a procedure; and he does so by focusing attention on the tale itself rather than the story.

Critical commentaries on this passage have usually centered attention on the physical juxtaposition of "inside" and "outside," as if "episode" were the pivot on which Conrad's distinction balances. As a matter of fact, the pivotal term is "tale." The episode's meaning is brought out by the tale, "as a glow brings out a haze." The telling, rather than the event itself, generates meaning. The "spectral illumination of moonshine" would then seem to stand for the inner vision which elaborates past experiences into memory and linguistic rendition, while the tale is the account to both an event and its effect on the writer. The frame narrator is drawing the reader's attention to the duality of Marlow's story. He warns his readers that they must not concentrate on Marlow's account of the events in which he is protagonist, but rather on the distortions which the re-creation of his subjective experience produces on the narrative. The "meaning" of the episode lies in the traces of how he experienced those events.

—Richard Ambrosini, *Conrad's Fiction as Critical Discourse* (Cambridge: Cambridge University Press, 1991), pp. 88–90

✣

OTTO BOHLMANN ON EXISTENTIALISM IN *HEART OF DARKNESS*

[Otto Bohlmann has written *Yeats and Nietzsche* (1982) and *Conrad's Existentialism* (1991), from which the following extract is taken. Here, Bohlmann probes the elements of existentialism and the influence of Nietzschean ideas in *Heart of Darkness*.]

The only valuable work, Marlow later suggests, is the existential kind that offers you 'the chance to find yourself. Your own reality—for yourself, not for others—what no other man can ever know'. Not that the novel offers much evidence of such existential work being available as anything more than a desideratum. It was certainly not given to the fireman on Marlow's river craft, who was condemned to the inauthentic existence of a 'useful' object. 'He ought to have been clapping his hands and stamping his feet on the bank', at one with his world; 'instead of which he was hard at work, a thrall to strange witchcraft, full of improving knowledge'. 'To look at him was as edifying as seeing a dog in a parody of breeches and a feather hat, walking on his hind-legs'. Even the station manager was a mere cipher (though by no means in the same demeaned category as the company slaves). One who 'originated nothing, he could keep the routine going—that's all', like the Nietzschean 'objective man' who does not know 'how to affirm or how to deny' (*Beyond Good and Evil*).

Marlow himself would gain a deeper apprehension of life only once he had moved beyond 'the idleness of a passenger', beyond the 'they' with whom he found no 'point of contact', beyond 'the uniform sombreness of the coast' and the 'world of straightforward facts' that 'seemed to keep [him] away from the truth of things, within the toil of a mournful and senseless delusion'. As the existentialists constantly emphasize, preoccupation with quotidian activities leaves little time for reflecting on what one's personal truths should be.

Yet the possibility of transcending inauthenticity is always present. Once more we recall Kierkegaard saying that man is ever 'in process of becoming', which, as Edmond Jaloux has broadly argued, is patently true of so many Conradian figures. The doctor who asked to measure Marlow's head as he set off for the Congo was of the same opinion; " 'and, moreover, the changes take place inside, you know' ". " 'It would be interesting for science to watch the mental changes of individuals, on the spot.' " But to an existentialist the physiology of an individual can never reveal his essence. As in his constant emphasis on the unfathomable mystery of Jim the individual, Marlow in *Heart of Darkness* repeatedly stresses the impossibility of knowing another's 'mineness'. He would second Sartre's contention that, because each of us is ultimately alone in the world, we are closed to a full understanding of and by any other fellow being—or, indeed, to absolute self-knowledge. 'It is impossible', says Marlow, 'to convey the life-sensation of any given epoch of one's existence—that which makes its truth, its meaning—its subtle and penetrating essence. It is impossible. We live, as we dream—alone'. Again we are reminded of Sartre's assertion that mankind has no shared essence, that each individual creates his own particular essence, left to make his own discoveries about the self he is at 'any given epoch of [his] existence'.

Marlow certainly recognized the inauthentic straits of his own life when he encountered a 'whirl of black limbs' on the river bank at an early stage of his journey, putting us in mind of the narrator in *Nostromo,* who remarks that 'it may safely be said that primitive man did not go to the trouble of inventing tortures. He was indolent and pure of heart. He brained his neighbour ferociously with a stone axe from necessity and without malice'. There is, though, a marked tension between the controlled tone in *Nostromo* and Marlow's articulation of a similar sentiment in language that is rampant with kinetic images and propelling syntax which convey the vibrancy of the free natives' unfettered jungle life, yet is infused with suspensions and question marks that suggest the speculative nature of his remarks, which are but uncertain gropings at explaining the unfathomable. In Marlow's words, the natives were not 'inhuman. . . . They howled and leaped, and spun, and made horrid faces; but what thrilled you was just the thought of their humanity . . . . Ugly. Yes, it was ugly enough; but if you were man enough you would admit to yourself that there was in you just the faintest trace of a response to that terrible frankness of that noise. . . . And why not? The mind of man is capable of anything—because everything is in it, all the past as well as all the future. What was there after all? Joy, fear, sorrow, devotion, valour, rage—who can tell?—but truth—truth stripped of its cloak of time. Let the fool gape and shudder—the man knows, and can look on without a wink. But he must at least be as much of a man as these on the shore. He must meet that truth with his own true stuff—with his own inborn strength. Principles won't do'.

These are sentiments that would be wholly endorsed by Nietzsche, whom Freud regarded as having looked more deeply into human nature than anyone before him. Nietzsche, who admired the Greeks' 'intellectual predilection for the hard, gruesome, evil, problematic aspect of existence (*The Birth of Tragedy*), has Zarathustra command mankind to '*become hard!'* Man's unblinking recognition of his conflicting impulses is in Nietzsche's estimation what gives him his capacity to create. 'One must still have chaos in one', remarks Zarathustra, 'to give birth to a dancing star'. 'For every strong and natural species of man, love and hate, gratitude and revenge, good nature and anger, affirmative acts and negative acts, belong together. One is good on condition one also knows how to be evil; one is evil because otherwise one would not understand how to be good' (*The Will to Power*). To become ' "good human beings", herd animals, blue-eyed, benevolent, "beautiful souls"—or as Mr Herbert Spencer would have it, altruistic—would deprive existence of its *great* character' (*Ecce Homo*). Zarathustra despises those 'who think themselves good because they have crippled paws'. The multiplicity of the human self—as manifold as that of the universe—cannot be reduced to systematic formulae; as we remember Nietzsche saying, 'I mistrust all systematizers and avoid them. The will to a system is a lack of integrity' (*Twilight of the Idols*).

Yet Nietzsche is painfully aware of the darker elements which infuse that multiplicity, what Whitman called the 'multitudes' he 'contained'. *The Birth of Tragedy* speaks of how terrible and revolting to current moral standards the deep urges in the hearts of men are: men have 'the most savage natural instincts . . . , including even that horrible mixture of sensuality and cruelty which has always seemed to me to be the real "witches' brew" '. 'Man rests, with the unconcern of his ignorance, on the pitiless, the ravenous, the insatiable, the murderous'. In him is 'matter, fragment, excess, clay, mud, madness, chaos; but in man there is also creator, sculptor, the hardness of the hammer, the divine spectator and the seventh day' (*Beyond Good and Evil*). It requires a robust psyche to acknowledge this, and Nietzsche's 'new barbarian . . . who comes from the heights', a Promethean 'barbarian', is bred of the 'noble caste', whose 'superiority lay, not in their physical strength, but primarily in their psychical—they were *more complete* human beings (which, on every level, also means as much as "more complete beasts"—)' (*Beyond Good and Evil*). They had the inner strength to confront the 'horrible truth' which in lesser men promotes lassitude (*The Birth of Tragedy*).

—Otto Bohlmann, *Conrad's Existentialism* (New York: St. Martin's Press, 1991), pp. 97–99

Graham Bradshaw on British Imperialism in *Heart of Darkness*

[Graham Bradshaw is a member of the English faculty at the University of St. Andrews in Scotland. He has written *Shakespeare's Skepticism* (1987) and *Misrepresentations: Shakespeare and the Materialists* (1993). In this extract, Bradshaw explores Conrad's use of British imperialism in *Heart of Darkness*.]

Turning to *Heart of Darkness,* there is no doubt about Conrad's attitude to the activities of Leopold II's rapacious agents in the Belgian Congo. But then the story's attitude to *British* imperialism is harder to determine, and this issue is foregrounded—before Marlow begins his tale proper, and before any mention of the Belgians—by Marlow's rather queer determination to praise the modern Britons at the expense of the ancient Romans. He first claims that 'What redeems us is efficiency—the devotion to efficiency'. Then, as if recognizing that there might indeed be some difficulty in explaining wherein the Romans were less 'efficient', or in presenting this difference as a *moral* difference, Marlow shifts his ground, to claim that what 'redeems us' is 'the idea only'—and then, instead of specifying the content of this 'idea', Marlow makes the idea sound more like an idol, saying that it has to be 'something you can set up, and bow down before, and offer a sacrifice to'. In *Sincerity and Authenticity* Lionel Trilling charged Conrad with ideological bias and bad faith, arguing that Conrad was trying to smuggle in some soothingly special exemption for the British, before launching into an indictment of the ideology of imperialism. But here, as in the examples of alleged bias in *Nostromo* and *The Secret Agent,* there is a misunderstanding of complex narrational and structural ironies.

This becomes clearer if we make those distinctions Trilling should have made—that is, if we distinguish not merely between Conrad and Marlow, but also between Marlow the narrator and Marlow the protagonist. In the passages which alarm Trilling Marlow the narrator is indeed attempting some kind of affirmation of cultural solidarity; moreover, the Marlow who assures his respectable friends and pillars of the Establishment that the Continent is 'cheap and not so nasty as it looks' is decidedly British, unlike the 'Continental' Conrad. Marlow is—in that phrase which runs through *Lord Jim*—'one of us'. But once Marlow the protagonist had found himself unable to 'keep my hold on the redeeming facts of life', being British seemed not to help very much. Instead of showing how Marlow the protagonist was sustained by 'efficiency', the first part of *Heart of Darkness* ends, tellingly, by showing how Marlow gave up his concern with 'rivets' and getting the job done: 'One's capacity for that kind of folly is more limited than you would suppose', observes Marlow the narrator. Neither is Marlow the protagonist sustained by some British 'idea': on the contrary, he has lost those assurances of the 'civilised crowd' which (as Conrad wrote in his other Congo story) 'believes blindly in the irresistible force of its institutions and of its morals, in the power of its police and of its opinions'. Significantly enough, Marlow the narrator angrily accuses his immediate audience of being unable to 'understand' these things:

> You can't understand. How could you?—with solid pavement under your feet, surrounded by kind neighbours ready to cheer you or to fall on you stepping delicately between the butcher and the policeman, in the holy terror of scandal and gallows and lunatic asylum . . .

Where, in this tirade, is that redeeming British 'idea'?

Here I must start pulling my various suggestions together. I have tried to isolate a particular kind of difficulty which confronts us when we try to establish from what standpoint *Nostromo, The Secret Agent* or *Heart of Darkness* offer seemingly firm particular judgments of issues and events. That difficulty can best be formulated, I suggest, in terms of the modern anthropologist's familiar distinction between *mythos,* or *world view,* and *ethos.* As Clifford Geertz puts it in *Islam Observed, world view* is the usual term for 'the collection of notions a people has of how reality is at base put together', while the people's 'general style of life, the way they do things and like to see things done', is called their *ethos.* Geertz then argues that the 'heart' of the religious perspective or way of looking at the world is not the theory that beyond the visible world lies an invisible one; not the doctrine that a divine presence broods over the world; but, rather, 'the conviction that the values one holds are grounded in the inherent structure of reality, that between the way one ought to live and the way things really are there is an unbreakable inner connexion'. So, what 'sacred symbols do for those to whom they are sacred is to formulate an image of the world's construction and a program for human conduct that are mere reflexes of one another', since *world view* and *ethos* are mutually confirming:

> Such symbols render the world believable and the ethos justifiable, and they do it invoking each in support of the other. The world view is believable because the ethos, which grows out of it, is felt to be authoritative; the ethos is justifiable because the world view, upon which it rests, is held to be true. Seen from outside the religious perspective, this sort of hanging a picture from a nail driven into its frame appears as a kind of sleight of hand. Seen from inside, it appears as a simple fact.

In Conrad, there is *no* corresponding conviction that 'the values one holds are grounded in the inherent structure of reality', and no 'unbreakable inner connexion' of the kind Geertz locates at the 'heart' of the 'religious perspective'. Those very narrational tensions which I have been wanting to isolate consistently accentuate a *rift* between *mythos* and *ethos,* between 'seeing from inside', in Geertz's sense, and 'seeing from outside'.

Hence Marlow's attack on his immediate audience for being unable to 'understand'. He assumes that his listeners will mistake their cultural values for objective values; will see their sustaining *mythos* as something ontologically true, grounded in the inherent structure of reality, not as a cultural product which sustains and is sustained by kind neighbours and lunatic asylums, policemen and . . . historians. Here we might compare that much quoted and (I think) much misunderstood passage in *Lord Jim* where Marlow broods over what makes Jim seem 'one of us'. Falteringly, and with *justified* misgivings, Marlow imagines that what is in question must be some 'inborn ability',

> a faith invulnerable to the strength of facts, to the contagion of example, to the solicitation of ideas. Hang ideas! They are tramps, vagabonds, knocking at the back-door of your mind, each taking away a little of your substance, each carrying away some crumb of that belief in a few simple notions you must cling to if you want to live decently and would like to die easy.

Characteristically, the Marlow of *Lord Jim,* like the Marlow of *Heart of Darkness,* will not surrender his concern to *live decently*—that is, his concern with *ethos,* or conduct. But once again a wedge is being driven between *mythos* and *ethos.* Far from being grounded in the inherent structure of reality, the 'few simple notions' are pathetically exposed to 'fact' or 'example' on the one hand, to 'ideas' on the other. What fragile little fictions are these? What could be more poignantly *in*substantial than a 'substance' which apparently cannot withstand either empirical or logical pressure? The 'faith' or 'belief' to which this troubled Marlow wants to 'cling' here resembles the 'faith' of Kurtz's fiancée, the so-called 'Intended', in *Heart of Darkness:* it is certainly not grounded in the inherent structure of reality, and is rather an illusion—but, and here the Nietzschean dilemma appears, it is an illusion which may sustain life where the truth would be 'too dark altogether'.

—Graham Bradshaw, "Mythos, Ethos, and the Heart of Conrad's Darkness," *English Studies* 72, No. 2 (April 1991): 166–68

RITA BODE ON THE WOMEN IN *HEART OF DARKNESS*

[Rita Bode is a professor of English at Trent University in Peterboro, Ontario, Canada. In this extract, Bode studies the elusive presence of women in *Heart of Darkness,* who seem to echo the obscurity of the African jungle into which Marlow penetrates.]

Time and again, Conrad's women seem to exercise control over the male characters. The theme of brotherhood, particularly as it plays itself out in the doubling of Marlow and Kurtz, has long been accepted as a fruitful approach to Conrad's work. But the women also form significant reflections of each other. The connections among them are many. They form a kind of sisterhood in which each female seems to support and complete the intents of the others. The men, however unwittingly, succumb to their will. The separate female space, which, according to Marlow, the women inhabit, becomes by the novella's end the dominant one, drawing within its parameters the male characters as well. I wish to suggest in this essay that present in *Heart of Darkness* is a powerful female network, which frequently takes charge and assumes control of the novella's events, of the Marlow who experiences the Congo, as well as the Marlow who tells the tale.

The argument, however, for such a female network exerting any power seems problematic. The brotherhood of Marlow and Kurtz, rooted in Marlow's conscious identification of himself with Kurtz, seems a very different matter from a "sisterhood" in which the women, on the narrative level, are unaware of each other's existence. The women in *Heart of Darkness,* indeed, appear to be functions of Marlow's (and Kurtz's) imagination, and as such, their status as autonomous individuals is shaky. Their powers appear questionable. And yet, the many connections among them are forceful enough to make the novella's women grow beyond, indeed, become too large for the imaginative constructs that try to contain them. The subtle, but powerful web of connections among the women belies Marlow's narrative to suggest a female presence and authority lying outside his interpretations. While some of the connections are made directly by Marlow himself, and others emerge through Kurtz's relationships, still others are highly suggestive metaphorical links, reflecting various degrees of Conrad's conscious artistry. The combination of these three modes of conveying the links among the women implies that, to some extent, Conrad overtly intends that there be a strong female presence in the work, while covertly he is perhaps grappling with this female presence as Marlow himself is. Marlow struggles to maintain his own limited image of womankind. He frequently protests too much, suggesting a basic uneasiness that the women might possibly have an existence beyond his interpretation of them. He consistently refuses to acknowledge or explore the implications of the links that he himself at times brings to our attention. Marlow's omission suggests that he fears these women. The narrative discrepancy between his easy dismissal of them and his unacknowledged fear, between his concept of women and the impression created by the novella's women suggests an independent context for them; but it is the intense textual connections that truly empower the women, for these create a kind of sub-text in *Heart of Darkness*—perhaps even a story within a story (one over which Marlow has no control)—that ripples suggestively throughout the narrative. My concern in this essay, then, is with this sub-text.

Marlow's assessment of the female condition is well-known. He tells us early on: " 'It's queer how out of touch with truth women are! They live in a world of their own and there had never been anything like it and never can be. It is too beautiful altogether, and if they were to set it up it would go to pieces before the first sunset. Some confounded fact, we men have been living contentedly with ever since the day of creation, would start up and knock the whole thing over.' " Marlow postulates the existence of a separate female space, limited in its vision, contained in its possibilities. For him, women exist in a world apart from "truth" and "fact." Yet if the women, as Marlow later states, are " 'out of it,' " then, so, too, is Marlow, himself, for in his journey up the Congo, he also enters a world in which truth and reality become difficult, if not impossible, to discern. Even as he moves toward the river, Marlow already feels himself kept away " 'from the truth of things within the toil of a mournful and senseless delusion.' " He also has to make a concerted effort to keep hold " 'on the redeeming facts of life.' " The physical world itself in the Congo, the fog, the darkness, the impenetrable jungle, severely limits discernment. " 'What was in there?' " Marlow wonders. There is, furthermore, no returning clarity with the return from the Congo. In his narration on the *Nellie,* the dream sensation is still strongly with him: " 'It seems to me I am trying to tell you a dream—making a vain attempt, because no relation of a dream can convey the dream-sensation, that commingling of absurdity, surprise and bewilderment in a tremor of struggling revolt, that notion of being captured by the incredible which is the very essence of dreams . . .' " Confronted by the jungle, Marlow, too, seems " 'out of touch with truth.' " In other words, he seems to enter a world which closely resembles his view of female experience. This association becomes particularly significant when we consider that the jungle itself is referred to consistently in female terms. Its embrace, its presence, its very soul are feminine. The wilderness "had caressed him . . . taken him, loved him, embraced him, got into his veins, consumed his flesh" runs Marlow's sensuous description of Kurtz. As Marlow makes explicitly clear, Kurtz's African mistress reflects the mighty female force of the jungle: " 'And in the hush that had fallen suddenly upon the whole sorrowful land, the immense wilderness, the colossal body of the fecund and mysterious life seemed to look at her, pensive, as though it had been looking at the image of its own tenebrous and passionate soul.' " Marlow's journey into the female jungle is more than a sexual allegory of male penetration; it is an immersion into a separate other world corresponding disturbingly to the female world which, on a conscious level, he dismisses. It is the nightmare underside of his " 'beautiful' " world of women, a nightmare, in part, at least, because he is forcefully drawn into what he had so confidently placed apart.

—Rita Bode, " 'They . . . Should Be Out of It': The Women of *Heart of Darkness*," *Conradiana* 26, No. 1 (Spring 1994): 20–22

✤

Books by Joseph Conrad

Almayer's Folly: A Story of an Eastern River. 1895.

An Outcast of the Islands. 1896.

The Nigger of the "Narcissus": A Tale of the Forecastle. 1897.

Tales of Unrest. 1898.

Lord Jim. 1900.

The Inheritors: An Extravagant Story (with Ford Madox Ford). 1901.

Youth: A Narrative, and Two Other Stories. 1902.

Typhoon. 1902.

Typhoon and Other Stories 1903.

Romance (with Ford Madox Ford). 1903.

Nostromo: A Tale of the Seaboard. 1904.

The Mirror of the Sea: Memories and Impressions. 1906.

The Secret Agent: A Simple Tale. 1907.

A Set of Six. 1908.

The Point of Honor: A Military Tale. 1908.

Under Western Eyes. 1911.

A Personal Record ⟨*Some Reminiscences*⟩. 1912.

'Twixt Land and Sea: Tales. 1912.

Chance. 1913.

Works (Deep Sea Edition). 1914. 24 vols.

Victory: An Island Tale. 1915.

Wisdom and Beauty from Conrad. Ed. M. Harriet M. Capes. 1915.

Within the Tides: Tales. 1915.

The Shadow-Line: A Confession. 1917.

One Day More. 1917.

"Well Done!" 1918.

Tradition. 1919.

The Arrow of Gold: A Story between Two Notes. 1919.

The Polish Question: A Note on the Joint Protectorate of the Western Powers and Russia. 1919.

The Shock of War. 1919.

Some Aspects of the Admirable Inquiry into the Loss of the Titanic. 1919.

To Poland in War-Time: A Journey into the East. 1919.

The Tale. 1919.

Prince Roman. 1920.

The Warrior's Soul. 1920.

The Rescue: A Romance of the Shallows. 1920.

Works (Sun-Dial Edition). 1920–25. 24 vols.

Notes on Life and Letters. 1921.

Notes on My Books. 1921.

The Secret Agent (drama). 1921.

The Black Mate. 1922.

The Rover. 1923.

Works (Uniform Edition). 1923–38. 22 vols.

The Nature of a Crime (with Ford Madox Ford). 1924.

Laughing Anne and One Day More: Two Plays. 1924.

Suspense: A Napoleonic Novel. 1925.

Tales of Hearsay. 1925.

Last Essays. Ed. Richard Curle. 1926.

Letters to His Wife. 1927.

Letters 1895–1924. Ed. Edward Garnett. 1928.

The Sisters. 1928.

Conrad to a Friend: 150 Selected Letters to Richard Curle. Ed. Richard Curle. 1928.

Lettres Françaises. Ed. Gerard Jean-Aubry. 1929.

The Book of Job: A Satirical Comedy by Bruno Winawer (translator). 1931.

Complete Short Stories. 1933.

Letters to Marguerite Poradowska 1890–1920. Ed. and tr. John Arthur Gee and Paul J. Sturm. 1940.

The Portable Conrad. Ed. Morton Dauwen Zabel. 1947.

Letters to William Blackwood and David S. Meldrum. Ed. William Blackburn. 1958.

Conrad's Polish Background: Letters to and from Polish Friends. Ed. Zdzislaw Najder. Tr. Halina Carroll. 1963.

Letters to R. B. Cunninghame Graham. Ed. C. T. Watts. 1969

Congo Diary and Other Uncollected Pieces. Ed. Zdzislaw Najder. 1978.

Collected Letters. Eds. Frederick R. Karl and Laurence Davies. 1983– . 8 vols. (projected).

Works (Cambridge Edition). Ed. S. W. Reid et al. 1989–

Interviews and Recollections. Ed. Martin Ray. 1990.

Complete Short Fiction. Ed. Samuel Hynes. 1991–92. 4 vols.

Works about Joseph Conrad, *Heart of Darkness*, and "The Secret Sharer"

Adelman, Gary. Heart of Darkness: *Search for the Unconscious.* Boston: Twayne, 1987.

Andreach, Robert J. *The Slain and Resurrected God: Conrad, Ford, and the Christian Myth.* New York: New York University Press, 1970.

Baines, Jocelyn. *Joseph Conrad: A Critical Biography.* New York: McGraw-Hill, 1960.

Batchelor, John. *The Life of Joseph Conrad: A Critical Biography.* Oxford: Basil Blackwell, 1994.

Bennett, Carl D. *Joseph Conrad.* New York: Continuum, 1991.

Berman, Jeffrey. *Joseph Conrad: Writing as Rescue.* New York: Astra Books, 1977.

Berthoud, Jacques. *Joseph Conrad: The Major Phase.* Cambridge: Cambridge University Press, 1978.

Bloom, Harold, ed. *Joseph Conrad's* Heart of Darkness. New York: Chelsea House, 1987.

———, ed. *Marlow.* New York: Chelsea House, 1992.

Bonney, William M. *Thorns and Arabesques: Contexts for Conrad's Fiction.* Baltimore: Johns Hopkins University Press, 1980.

Bruss, Paul. *Conrad's Early Sea Fiction: The Novelist as Navigator.* Lewisburg, PA: Bucknell University Press, 1979.

Cooper, Christopher. *Conrad and the Human Dilemma.* London: Chatto & Windus, 1970.

Crews, Frederick. "The Power of Darkness." *Partisan Review* 34 (1967): 507–25.

Daleski, H. M. *Joseph Conrad, the Way of Dispossession.* New York: Holmes & Meier, 1977.

Dowden, Wilfred S. *Joseph Conrad: The Imaged Style.* Nashville: Vanderbilt University Press, 1970.

Erdinast-Vulcan, Daphna. *Joseph Conrad and the Modern Temper.* Oxford: Clarendon Pess, 1991.

Fleishman, Avrom. *Conrad's Politics.* Baltimore: Johns Hopkins Press, 1967.

Fogel, Aaron. *Coercion to Speak: Conrad's Poetics of Dialogue.* Cambridge, MA: Harvard University Press, 1985.

Ford, Ford Madox. *Joseph Conrad: A Personal Remembrance.* Boston: Little, Brown, 1924.

Gekoski, R. A. *Conrad: The Moral World of the Novelist.* New York: Barnes & Noble. 1978.

Glassman, Peter J. *Language and Being: Joseph Conrad and the Literature of Personality.* New York: Columbia University Press, 1976.

Graham, Kenneth. *Indirections of the Novel: James, Conrad, and Forster.* Cambridge: Cambridge University Press, 1988.

Hampson, Robert. *Joseph Conrad: Betrayal and Identity.* New York: St. Martin's Press, 1992.

Hansford, James. "Closing, Enclosure and Passage in 'The Secret Sharer.' " *Conradian* 15 (1990): 30–55.

Haugh, Robert F. *Joseph Conrad: Discovery in Design.* Norman: University of Oklahoma Press, 1957.

Hawkins, Hunt. "Conrad's Critique of Imperialism in *Heart of Darkness.*" *PMLA* 94 (1979): 286–99.

Hawthorn, Jeremy. *Joseph Conrad: Language and Fictional Self-Consciousness.* Lincoln: University of Nebraska Press, 1979.

Hendricksen, Bruce. *Nomadic Voices: Conrad and the Subject of Narrative.* Urbana: University of Illinois Press, 1992.

Jean-Aubry, Georges. *The Sea-Dreamer: A Definitive Biography of Joseph Conrad.* Garden City, NY: Doubleday, 1957.

Johnson, Bruce. *Conrad's Models of Mind.* Minneapolis: University of Minnesota Press, 1971.

Karl, Frederick R. *Joseph Conrad, the Three Lives: A Biography.* New York: Farrar, Straus & Giroux, 1979.

Kirschner, Paul. *Conrad: The Psychologist as Artist.* Edinburgh: Oliver & Boyd, 1968.

Land, Stephen K. *Paradox and Polarity in the Fiction of Joseph Conrad.* New York: St. Martin's Press, 1984.

Leavis, F. R. *The Great Tradition: George Eliot, Henry James, Joseph Conrad.* London: Chatto & Windus, 1948.

Leondopoulous, Jordan. *Still the Moving World: Intolerance, Modernism, and* Heart of Darkness. New York: Peter Lang, 1991.

London, Bette. *The Appropriated Voice: Narrative Authority in Conrad, Foster, and Woolf.* Ann Arbor: University of Michigan Press, 1990.

Lothe, Jakob. *Conrad's Narrative Method.* Oxford: Clarendon Press, 1989.

McLauchlan, Juliet. "The 'Value' and 'Significance' of *Heart of Darkness.*" *Conradiana* 15 (1983): 3–21.

Morf, Gustav. *The Polish Heritage of Joseph Conrad.* New York: Richard R. Smith, 1930.

Moser, Thomas C. *Joseph Conrad: Achievement and Decline.* Cambridge, MA: Harvard University Press, 1957.

Murfin, Ross C., ed. *Conrad Revisited: Essays for the Eighties.* University: University of Alabama Press, 1985.

Navarette, Susan J. "The Anatomy of Failure in Joseph Conrad's *Heart of Darkness.*" *Texas Studies in Literature and Language* 35 (1993): 279–315.

Nettels, Elsa. *James and Conrad.* Athens: University of Georgia Press, 1977.

Paccaud, Josiane. "Under the Other's Eyes: Conrad's 'The Secret Sharer.' " *Conradian* 12 (1987): 59–73.

Page, Norman. *A Companion to Conrad.* New York: St. Martin's Press, 1986.

Parry, Benita. *Conrad and Imperialism.* London: Macmillan, 1983.

Raval, Suresh. *The Art of Failure: Conrad's Fiction.* London: Allen & Unwin, 1986.

Ressler, Steve. *Joseph Conrad: Consciousness and Integrity.* New York: New York University Press, 1988.

Rising, Catharine. *Darkness at Heart: Fathers and Sons in Conrad.* Westport, CT: Greenwood Press, 1990.

Schwarz, Daniel R. *Conrad,* Almayer's Folly *to* Under Western Eyes. Ithaca, NY: Cornell University Press, 1980.

Seltzer, Leon F. *The Vision of Melville and Conrad: A Comparative Study.* Athens: Ohio University Press, 1970.

Shaffer, Brian W. " 'Rebarbarizing Civilization': Conrad's African Fiction and Spencerian Sociology." *PMLA* 108 (1993): 45–58.

Sherry, Norman. *Conrad's Eastern World.* Cambridge: Cambridge University Press, 1966.

Spittles, Brian. *Joseph Conrad: Text and Context.* New York: St. Martin's Press, 1992.

Stallman, R. W., ed. *The Art of Joseph Conrad: A Critical Symposium.* East Lansing: Michigan State University Press, 1960.

Thorburn, David. *Conrad's Romanticism.* New Haven: Yale University Press, 1974.

Watt, Ian. *Conrad in the Nineteenth Century.* Berkeley: University of California Press, 1979.

Watts, Cedric. *Joseph Conrad: A Literary Life.* New York: St. Martin's Press, 1989.

Wollaeger, Mark A. *Joseph Conrad and the Fictions of Skepticism.* Stanford: Stanford University Press, 1990.

Index of Themes and Ideas